Violet
Last Rites

Rob Ryder

Ojai, California

Copyright © 2014 Rob Ryder
www.FriendsofViolet.com

ISBN: 978-0-9909034-0-6

Cover and Interior Design by Steven W. Booth
(This guy is every writer's best friend.)
www.GeniusBookServices.com

Dedication

To the caregivers. The angels. The invisible ones who become so important as our aging parents—as we—fall into need.

So, to them. The quiet givers, with their big hearts and their tough souls.

April 12, 2014

My Mom calls to tell me she stopped eating Tuesday. That's four days ago. But she says she isn't ready to leave us. (We talk frankly about death and dying. How and when she'll go.) But none of that today.

She's 95, in assisted-living at The Gables in Ojai, California. I'm lucky enough to live close by. On the drive over, I buy her a strong cup of coffee and big slice of New York cheesecake. It takes her a while but she eats the whole thing. Then she talks and talks.

April 13

What a difference a day makes (plus some New York cheesecake)! Although she's still not really eating.

"I had the most beautiful dream," Violet says. "I was living by myself, but surrounded by family and friends. I made everyone a big meal of lamb chops and mashed potatoes and carrots and peas and baby onions. Everyone ate every last bite and said it was the best meal they ever had!"

April 14

Violet calls me this morning.

"Something isn't right. I'm still not hungry."

"Let's get you to the doctor."

"Okay."

So I call and they say they can squeeze us in. Seems that her regular doctor, Dr. Nelson, is on vacation. The back-up doc can't find anything, so off we go to the lab for tests.

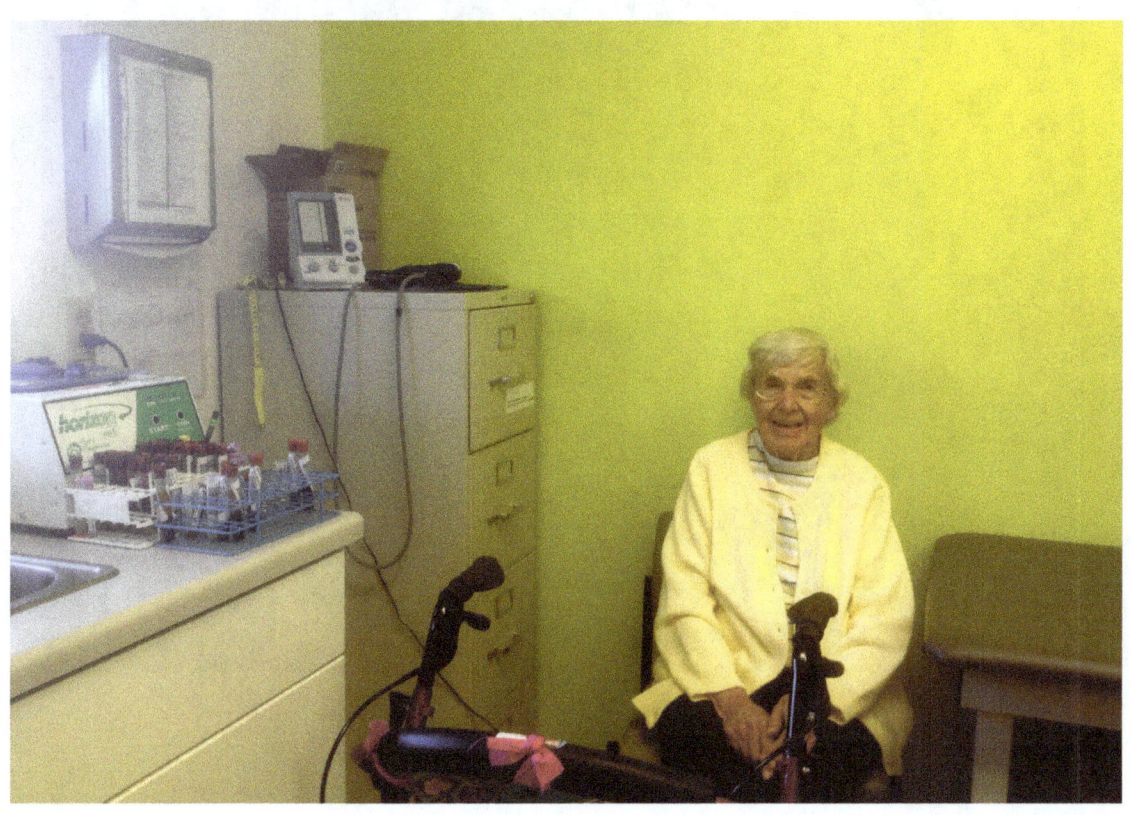

April 15

Awaiting the lab results. Violet's still not eating. She nibbles and sips cranberry juice. But no hunger, no pain. So we stroll outside, have a few laughs and take a selfie:

April 16

Violet and I sit together in her room. I ask for a story from the past to get our minds off the present. Violet tells me this about my Polish grandfather:

"It was Easter Sunday 1950. My father was very sick. He got up early and walked alone to 6 a.m. Mass. Then he went home. This was in Brooklyn. I left your brothers with your father and went to visit him. He was back in bed. He held my hand and said, 'I'm going now, but it's okay. Someone new is arriving to replace me.' I was crying. I didn't know what he meant. He died in his sleep later that day. I didn't even know I was pregnant. But you were born that November."

April 17

The doctor calls. The tests came out negative. But Violet hasn't eaten in a week. She's lost over 10 pounds. We schedule an ultrasound. The first spot available is in three days. Violet and I sit quietly.

"Rob, there's something wrong with me. It's not like I'm just giving up. I'm not."

"Yeah, so they'll find it, and then we'll deal with it."

She looks at me, her eyes clear. "I don't want any sugarcoating. We'll promise to tell each other the truth, even if it's hard."

"Promise," I say.

April 18

Violet brightens up this morning when I finally tell her about her loyal Facebook fans. (I've been posting pics and anecdotes about her for the last few years.) She says hi to all. And she seems happy enough to smile for the camera—maybe because it's an iPhone and less obtrusive.

"Mom, looking at you, I know you're not eating, but you actually look pretty good. I don't think you're ready to die here."

"Sometimes I wonder. We'll see what tomorrow brings…"

Ten minutes later she asks me if maybe she could move to a larger room. That's what she needs! Her fifth move in six years (she kept finding nicer apartments at The Gables). Yet another move, that'll keep her goin'…

April 19

Waiting. Worried. I ask Violet for more from her past. It seems that my devoutly Catholic, Polish grandparents refused to allow it when my agnostic, socialist Norwegian father asked my Mom to marry him. So my Dad took off for Alaska and wrote Violet to come join him. Her parents caught her packing her bags. They sent my Uncle Witold instead. Witold took a train to Seattle, then a steamer up to Anchorage, then a bus to Fairbanks where he somehow found my father. Witold was 17 at the time. He told my father that if he wanted to marry my mother he'd better come back to Brooklyn. So he did, and they were married in 1942.

April 20

Easter Sunday. My younger son Andre stops by to visit. He tells Violet about his new purpose in life, the organic farm he works on here in the Ojai Valley. Their goat had two kids. And their 60 laying hens produce dozens of speckled eggs every day.

    I say, "Mom, maybe Andre can bring you an egg that we can soft-boil for you to eat."

    "I could try," she says. "At least I could taste it."

    Andre says goodbye and Violet and I just sit there, looking out the window. Birds flit around her birdfeeder. She's antsy, and I take that for a good sign.

    "Let's go someplace," she says. "It's Easter."

"Okay, I've got an idea." So I get her to my car (no small feat) and we cruise through the Wendy's drive-up window and order fish sandwiches and fries. She nibbles at a fry as I drive across the valley up to Thacher School. A favorite bench, facing the sun, with a beautiful view looking west over the Ojai Valley. I eat, she nibbles, we talk and enjoy the sun. Then my son Cole arrives from UCLA and plays his vintage guitar for her.

Overall, a good Easter. Ultrasound tomorrow.

April 21

Mystery solved! A single large gallstone gumming up the works. Here's Violet with the beautiful ultrasoundinista, Halena from Belarus.

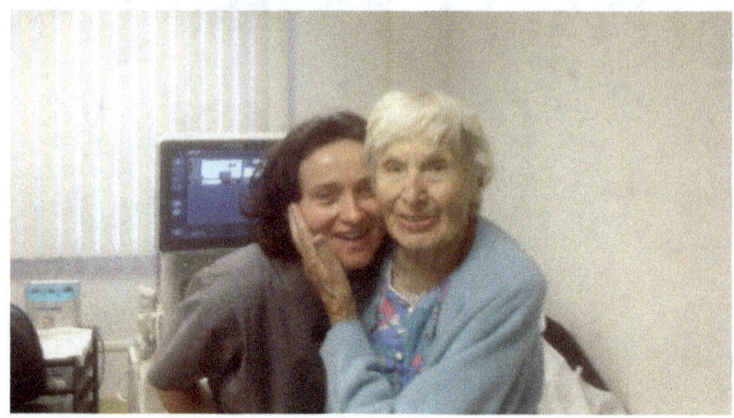

Violet and I are almost giddy with relief. I make an appointment with Dr. Davis, the gall bladder specialist.

April 22

Violet awakens with a sense of calm. I visit for just a few minutes—we need a little break from each other. So we each coast through the day in our own way.

April 23

A sudden dark turn when we visit the veteran Dr. Davis. He checks the pictures, discusses the gallstone, then probes deep with his fingers around Violet's gall bladder and abdomen. He frowns. "I don't like this."

"What is it?" asks Violet. (Unlike many patients, she's learned to interrogate her doctors until she knows as much about her condition as they do.)

Dr. Davis is wise and straightforward. "There's a large hard mass just below your stomach. I don't like the feel of it. Let's get you in for a CAT scan."

So off for a CAT scan we go. Hospital workers are angels. But a cloud hangs over the procedure, and the look on this angel's face is filled with unspoken sorrow.

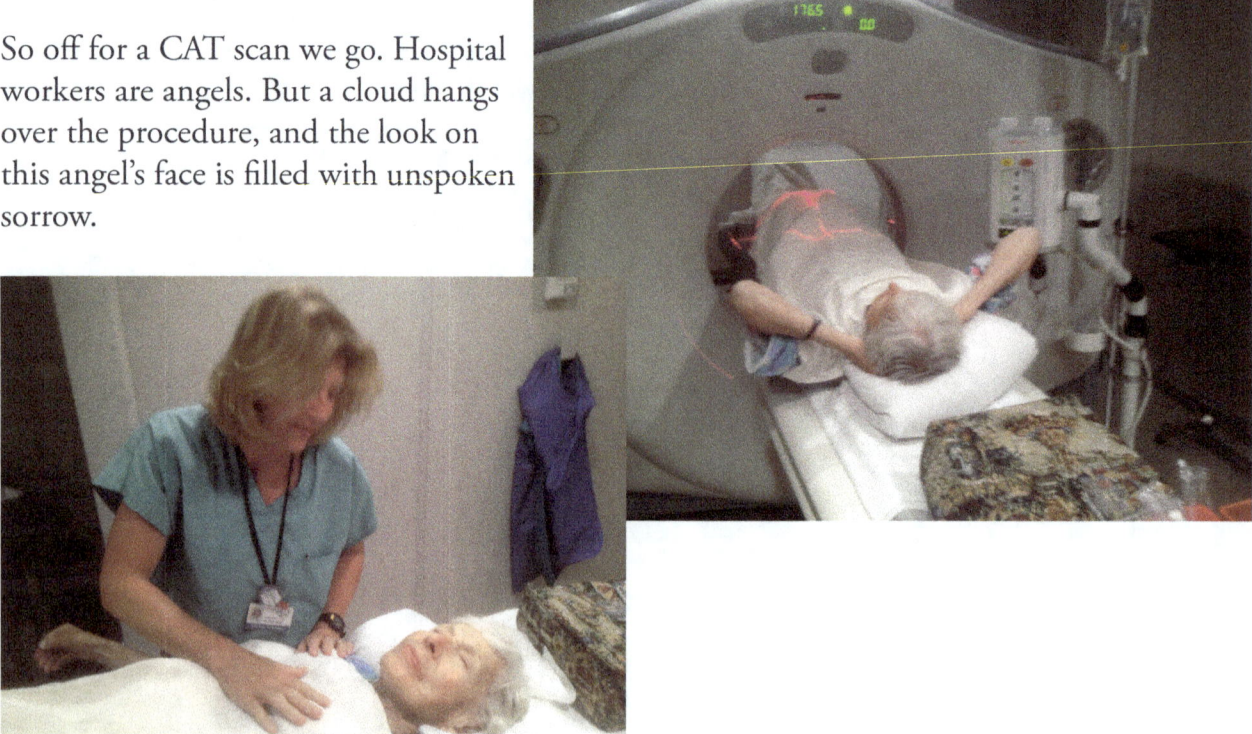

It's a quiet drive back to The Gables. The sun is setting, the sky all lit up. Normally Violet would comment. Not today.

"So it doesn't look good," I say.

"No."

"But we don't know for sure."

"Rob, it's not good."

"You seem to be holding up well. Are you okay?"

She thinks for a moment. "I've lived a long life. I've lived a good life." She smiles as we drive past some kids horsing around in front of Ojai Pizza.

"I've lived a life filled with life."

April 24

Dr. Davis calls me at 8 am. A brief, no-nonsense conversation. He ends with, "Should I tell her or do you want to?"

"I'll tell her."

I pick Violet up and we drive out again to the Thacher School overlook. She's very frail as I help her from the car to the bench. Her ribs pressing through her light sweater and house dress.

"Mom, I just talked to Dr. Davis. You have terminal cancer."

"They can't fix it?"

"No. They can try chemotherapy…"

"I don't want that."

"I think that's smart."

Her eyes brim with tears. The first I've seen in many years. They do not spill.

"Okay then."

April 25

Violet is thoughtful, reflective. "We should let people know."

"We'll get to it, Mom."

"I'm not happy about this. It's still not sinking in."

Later, I talk to Betsy, the terrific director of The Gables, about Violet's reaction.

"Family members forget," she says. "Just because someone's really old doesn't make it any easier for them to let go. Look, your mother's been having a wonderful life."

"Yeah," I say. "But we've talked about death. The inevitability of it."

"But that's not the same as getting the news."

"Yeah."

April 26

Violet is processing. Coming to terms. She always brightens when I ask about her past, so that's what I do.

"We didn't know we were poor. When we were kids in Brooklyn. We spoke Polish at home. My mother never really learned English. We had no television of course. Or telephone. The mail came twice a day. It was the 1920s. My uncle had a radio and all the men would listen to the fights. We had no refrigerator so they would deliver ice in big blocks for the ice box. I used to empty the drip pan every day. There were still horses and wagons in the streets and horse poop everywhere. We went to Catholic school and the nuns were very good teachers but very strict. I missed only one half of one day for my entire schooling. If you were bad the nuns would smack your hand with a ruler. But they were mostly very nice. They wore habits. But they didn't ride bicycles."

Two days pass. I see Violet summoning the courage and grace to die right.

April 29

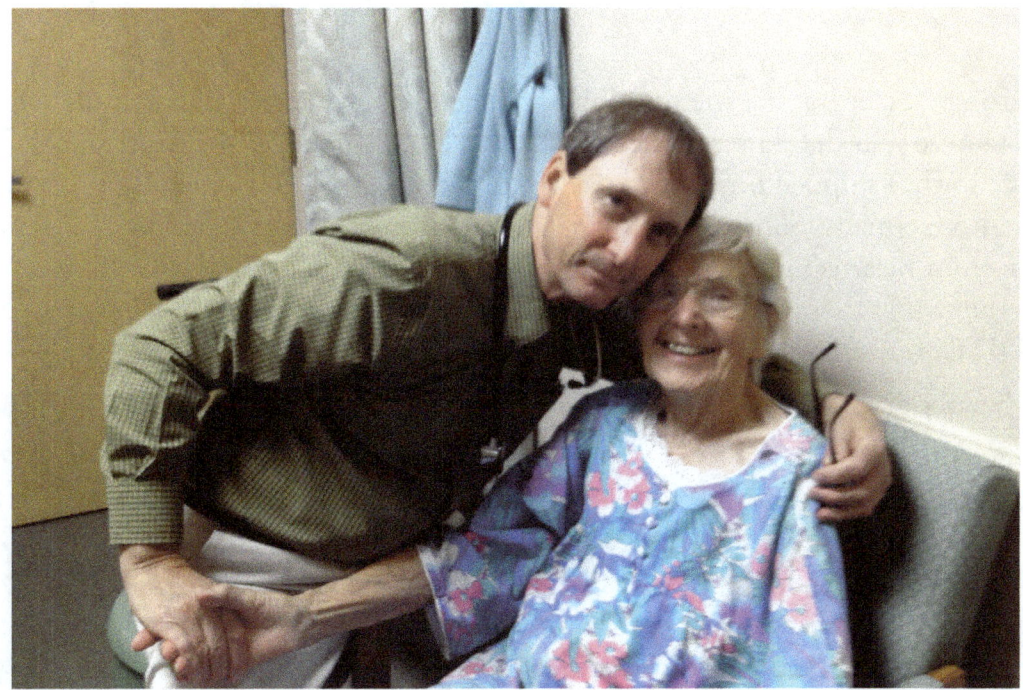

Dr. Nelson is back at work, and my Mom pays a final visit as he transitions her to hospice care. The decision is made, no IVs, no feeding tubes. DNR – Do Not Resuscitate.

He says, "Violet, if you can't eat, then make sure to drink plenty of fluids." (She's now lost almost 20 pounds.)

"Including alcohol?" I ask.

"Why not?"

I turn, "Mom, you've been so moderate your whole life, I'm gonna buy you a bottle of vodka and every evening we can make you a cocktail. Like cranberry juice, sparkling water, ice, lime, and a shot of Stoli. How's that sound?"

Violet considers, then smiles. "Maybe I'll turn into a real boozer."

April 30

She's getting weaker but her memory, ah… "When your father was drafted they sent him to Colorado to join the ski patrol because he was Norwegian. But he never skied a day in his life so they shipped him to France. He drove a road grader when the front lines pushed into Germany. Somehow a Russian joined him for the ride. I think he was a White Russian, from Belarus maybe. France was filled with Russian émigrés who wanted to fight Hitler. The two of them were quite the pair. Dad hung a sign on the road grader - SON OF A DITCH. All the soldiers got a laugh when they drove by."

"And what about the record he made over there?"

"Oh, yes. Later on he went to Paris on leave. He had written a song for me and he found one of those booths where you could sing into a microphone and they pressed a record for you. He wrapped it up and sent it to me. It was quite beautiful."

"I remember as a teenager finding it in the attic in New Jersey," I say. "A big heavy 78. I played it on our old record player. It surprised me. He was very talented."

"Yes."

"And romantic."

"Yes."

May 1

"My full name? You mean the name my parents first gave me?"

"Yes."

"Valentina Natalia Lyczkowski."

May 2

Angels in America. Violet's care providers. In addition to The Gables' staff, Violet now has a nurse, a chaplain, and social workers from Livingston Memorial hospice care.

They discuss coordinating schedules—showers, meals, medications, hearing aids, diapers, her religious beliefs, family visits, DNR…all of it. A solid hour of note taking and decision-making.

Betsy, the director, asks, "Anything else?"

"Yeah, her teeth," I say. "She's very self-conscious when her bridge isn't in."

"That's true," says Mariah.

"So that should be first thing, when she wakes up," I say. "That's the real reason she slept on the floor the night she fell. She didn't want anyone to see her without all her teeth in."

I stop by Violet's room after the meeting.

"Mom, you're gonna have a small army taking care of you now. They're bringing in the heavy artillery."

"That's nice," she says.

May 3

The days become a blur. I've taken to driving by The Gables late at night. If her light is on, I'll stop in. The light is on.

"You look sad tonight, Mom."

"I am."

"Okay. But tonight let's have a laugh. Tell me the funniest thing that ever happened to you."

She thinks and thinks. Finally a smile.

"It was at a high school outing. Aunt Rosalie and I and two other girls took a rowboat out into the middle of a muddy lake. Suddenly the rowboat sprung a leak. One of the girls panicked; she couldn't swim. We were yelling for help but the girls on the shore just waved to us. The boat was going under, so we all held hands and jumped overboard. But the lake was maybe two feet deep, so we were just standing there in the water! We laughed so hard we cried. The girls on the shore thought we were nuts."

May 4

Violet grows weaker. Barely able to eat at all now. In no pain. Mostly sleeping. But amazingly lucid when awake. Today we talk about my younger brother Mark. The youngest of us four boys.

"Mom, you didn't expect to get pregnant, did you?"

"Oh no. As a Catholic I practiced the rhythm method. It worked well because my periods were so regular. But Mark…he just wanted to be born. Your father was furious with me."

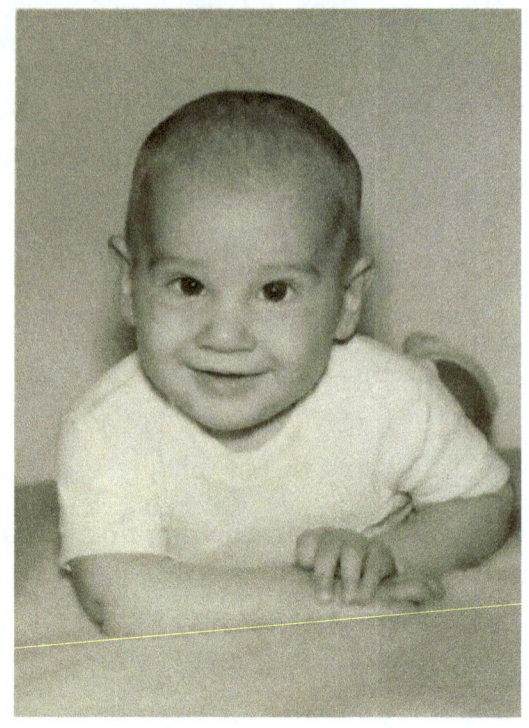

(My father was agnostic, known to mutter about "those damn priests.")

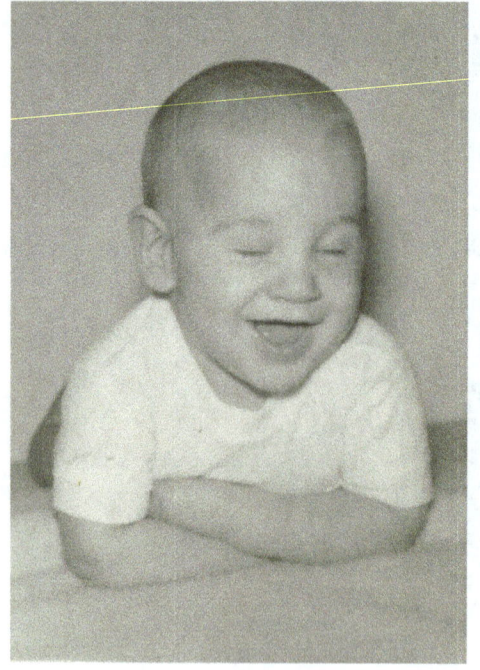

"He didn't speak to me for two months. Then on Valentine's Day, our anniversary, he brought me a box of chocolates. His way of reconciling. I threw it at him. But that broke the ice."

"And Mark was born that August."

"Yes. He was a beautiful baby. So filled with life and love. He melted every heart, including your father's."

"And he was 18 months old when he died?"

"Yes. From meningitis. I think about him every day. Picturing what a wonderful man he would have become."

"And he would have been what, 58 years old this August."

"Yes."

"You'll be with him soon."

"Yes."

May 5

Rough morning—Violet is quietly agitated.

"I had the most frustrating dream. I was stuck in some place and I was trying to get out but everything was moving around me and I couldn't find the exit. Then Rosalie was there (her sister who's been dead for years) but she couldn't help me…and that's all I remember." She falls silent.

"Mom, Father Fernando is coming today."

"Good. I didn't like that chaplain."

"I know. He was a substitute for the nice one. He won't be back. Plus Father Peter said he can come Thursday."

"Good."

"I remember when Dad was dying," I say. "At the VA hospital. I showed up late one night and there was some pompous guy talking at him about heaven and sin and redemption and Dad motioned me close and guess what he whispered to me."

"What?" she asks.

"Get this guy outta here. He's a horse's ass."

Violet smiles…

The cloud lifts, the day picks up. While I'm out, the young priest, Father Fernando, shows up to pray and administer The Last Rites.

"He cried," Violet tells me later. "He's very sensitive."

Then our dear friend Pamie arrives with a cheesecake and we have a little party, and Violet is able to eat a raspberry. She smiles and laughs. Then tonight, after a long nap, another story spills out.

"After Mark died, the UN assigned Dad to a post in Italy, and we all went over." (We were to stay four years in the seaside town of Tirrenia, just down from Pisa.)

"It was a real change. Suddenly we were living in a big house, and I had a full-time cook and housekeeper and your father had a fancy new black Cadillac, with two United Nations flags mounted on the front and a chauffeur who wore a uniform. All this for two poor kids from Brooklyn who never even went to college!"

"The cook was Bruna," I say.

"Yes…we became very close. But she couldn't understand when I got down to scrub the floors with her. But that was just who we were."

"And Dad?"

"Your father, the very first day, moved up and sat alongside the driver…I forget his name, but he was very handsome and dapper. And then Dad told him to forget about the uniform so he showed up in these nice Italian knit shirts and loafers, and soon he had Dad dressing like that."

"Sweet."

"And sometimes on Sundays when we were in church the two of them would drive up and down the coast, listening to the radio and smoking cigars."

May 6

A much better morning. Violet actually eats a soft-boiled egg and some watermelon. She says hi to all.

"Rob, you know I want to be cremated."

"It's all arranged."

"And buried alongside your father in Gold Hill."

"Yeah. We'll have a nice simple ceremony."

Back in the '70s my brothers and I designed and built a house for our parents in the Colorado Mountains. They were on assignment in Cyprus at the time, my Dad helping to separate the Greeks and the Turks. Although they eventually moved to California because of his health problems, my parents' hearts remained in Colorado, and soon they'll be there together.

"Mom, when we flew back to Colorado with Dad's ashes do you remember if we carried the box on the plane or did we check it?"

"I don't remember. I did gift wrap it though."

"That's right. But I'll probably have to check you into baggage, or they'll think I'm a terrorist."

"They'll think I'm a bomb!"

We laugh.

"And they'll be right," I say. "Because everyone on Facebook thinks you're da bomb."

Violet gives me a look.

May 6

An unexpected visit from Father Peter. He's called the zen priest by some. Perfect. They pray, then discuss her service—the music she wants, the words… It is very comforting to her. And before Father Peter leaves, he leans over her and performs a beautiful blessing, touching her with the sign of the cross at the end. Her face floods with light and love.

May 7

My brothers Paul and Ken arrive from Montana for a final visit. We all want to reminisce, but Violet first puts her den mother cap on—bank accounts, living trust, which clothes to Goodwill…

"And Father Peter knows a good mortuary for the cremation. Very reasonable."

"Mom, please… I already talked to one."

"How much is it?" she asks.

"Mom…"

"How much?"

"695 dollars."

"That's a lot of money. Maybe Father Peter's is cheaper."

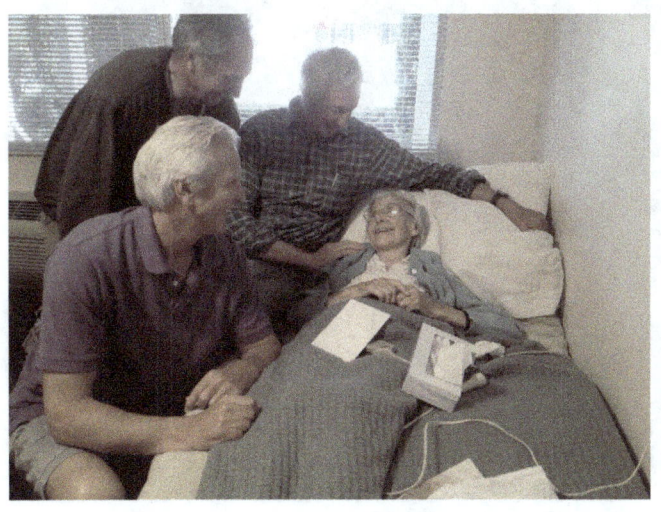

Ken jumps in, "Mom…"

But she won't let it go until finally I say, "Hey, you want to save money, I can buy a can of gasoline and we'll do it in the back yard."

Violet thinks for a moment. My brothers and I share a look of alarm.

Paul says, "Mom, he's joking!"

She laughs. "I know that!"

May 8

"Your father was a great dancer. When we lived in Europe there were lots of social events, and all the other ladies insisted on dancing with him. But he always saved the last dance for me."

May 8

Violet's fading. Sleeping more and more. Paul and Ken visit every few hours between naps. This afternoon, as we walk from Violet's room, a caregiver, Renee, pulls us aside.

"Can I tell you something?"

"Sure."

"When your Mom found out her condition, she called us into her room. One by one. All the caregivers. Over—it must have been two days and nights. And she had us sit down, and she held our hands, and she told us that she was dying, and that she would work with us to make it as good as possible. And I told her no, for you, we'll make it good for you, and she said no, for everyone, because we're all in this together."

Renee and Rosa

May 9

Violet receives a morning visit from her three sons. We talk of our time in Italy.

"That was so good for all of us," says Violet. "And the Italians loved us Americans."

Ken says, "It wasn't so long after World War II. We were the good guys."

Violet's eyes are shining. "And they loved President Kennedy. He was Catholic, of course. But they loved the style and they loved Jackie."

Paul says, "Remember how many times we climbed the Leaning Tower?"

"Oh, boy. But mostly," says Violet, "it was good for your Dad and me."

"What I remember best," I say, "Was whenever Tony DiMarco and I got hungry, we'd just ride our bikes to a trattoria and order tortellini and Coca-Cola in wine glasses, and it was the best tortellini. The best."

I stop by this afternoon as my brothers take a much-needed break at the beach. Violet's sitting up in a sleeveless nightgown. Her face is still full and radiant but her arms have become painfully thin. She notices me noticing.

"My arms are like sticks."

We make our way outside to sit in the sun. I ask about our move to the tract house in New Jersey in the early 1950s.

"It was brand new, and it felt like a mansion. Three bedrooms, a full basement, my own washing machine. We hung the clothes on a line to dry…"

"But just that one bathroom."

"But with a bathtub and a shower. And the yard for you boys."

"The neighborhood was filled with kids," I said.

"Especially after the Sirenos moved next door."

We laugh.

Devout Catholics, the Sirenos had a kid every year, finally stopping at eleven. All in a three bedroom, one bathroom house.

"It drove your father nuts, but he never said a mean word to them. And Peg became my best friend. She was very kind, and a wonderful singer. Remember how she would call her kids from outside by singing their names? Like opera almost."

The memory washes over us: Ma-a-a-a-ry! Jo-o-o-o-o-seph!

I say, "And Mrs. Friedman across the street would come out and sing her kids' names."

Er-i-ca-a-a-a! Ro-chel-el-el-el-el!

"It was quite beautiful," Violet says. "And those Sireno children, they learned to take care of each other. One day I went over, we never knocked, and Joey was giving the new baby a bath. Joey couldn't have been more than five years old at the time."

"And how their septic tank was always overflowing. That's what really drove Dad nuts. That smell."

"But their backyard had the greenest grass in New Jersey."

Violet is too weak to lift her curling iron, so my wonderful ex-wife, Andrea, comes by to help out. Voilà!

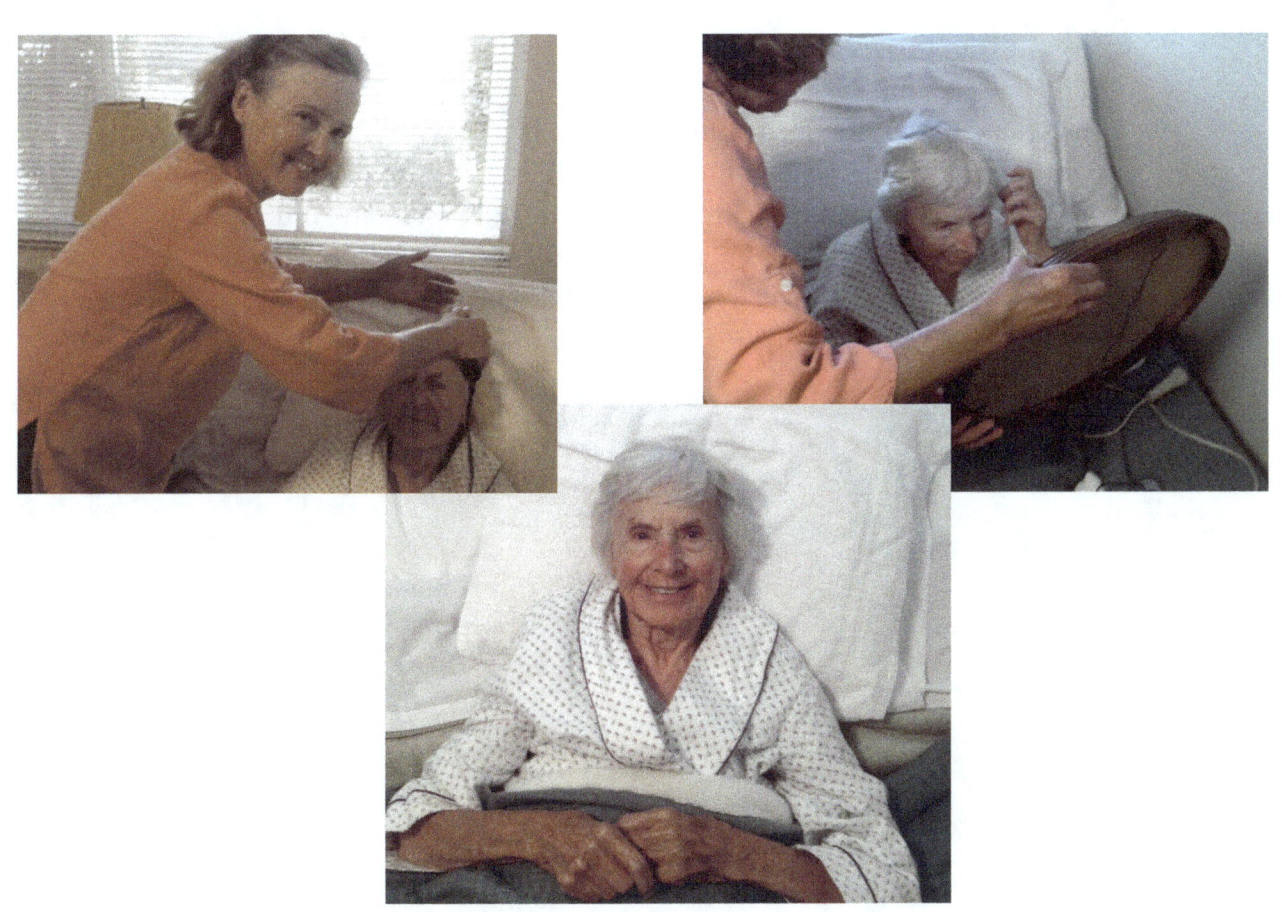

May 9

Violet and her firstborn, Paul, say their final farewell. Both my brothers are builders in Montana. Paul's current project is at a critical juncture and he must return. Tears for Violet. And a long drive back to Bozeman for Paul in his VW van. He'll be camping along the way, underneath the stars and a waxing moon.

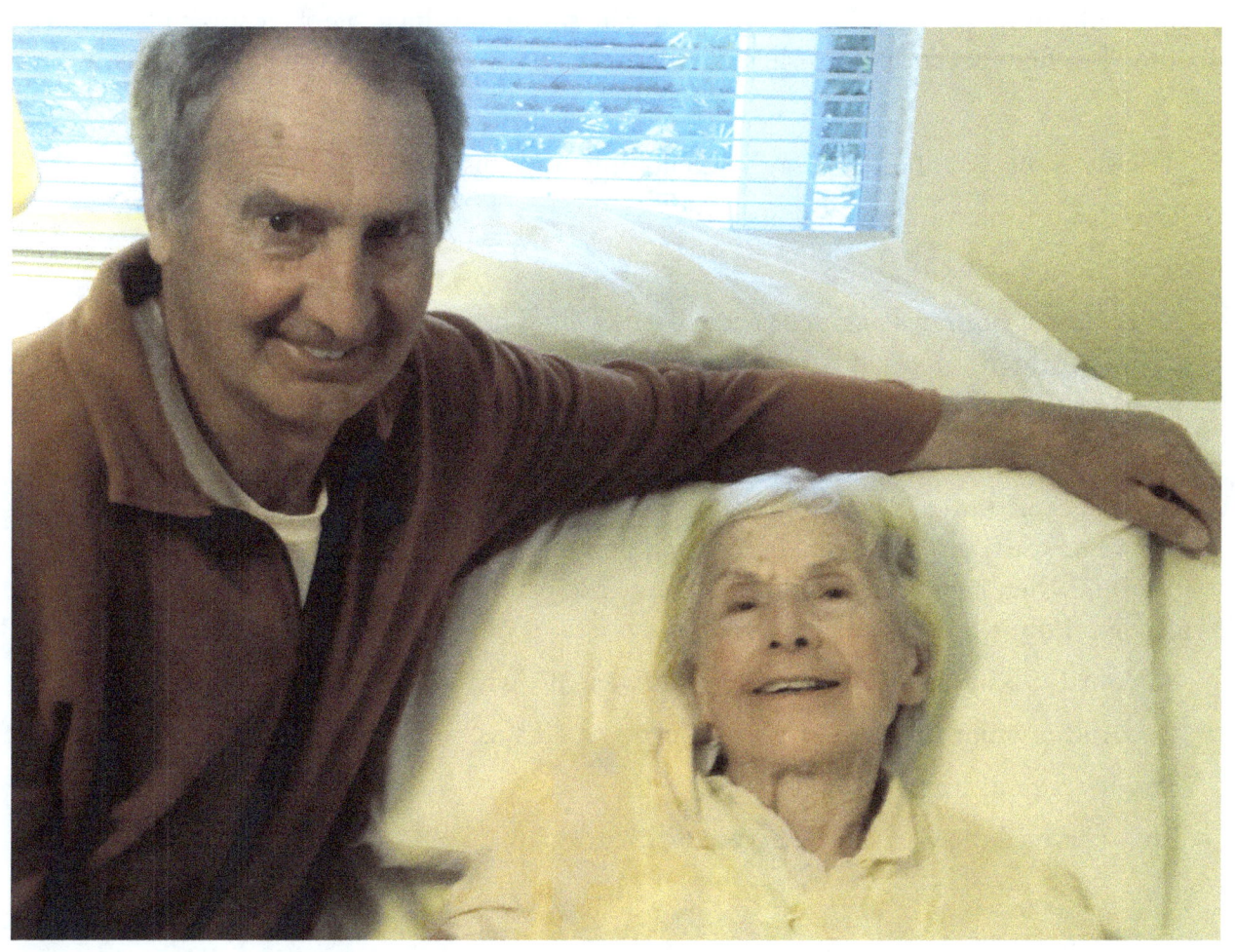

May 9

Violet looks beautiful in the afternoon light. She sips some ginger ale. Her speech has grown halting, but her eyes are clear as she talks about the past.

"Tell me about your father," I say. "I could only find this picture of your parents."

"Oh, this is from much later. Coney Island."

"Start at the beginning."

"Well, he was born in Poland, of course. In 1900. When he was 15, the war had already begun, World War I…and he was going to be drafted, so his mother put him on a ship to New York."

"By himself? Did he know anybody?"

"No. He came through Ellis Island alone. But there was a Polish woman in Brooklyn who took in new arrivals. She helped them find jobs, get on their feet, and that's what she did for him. When he met my mother they were both still teenagers and very quickly they got married. I don't think they even dated."

"So your Dad, my Polish grandfather, was what, 17 when Aunt Rosalie was born."

"Yes. And my mother maybe a year younger. And I was born a year later."

"And his parents back in Poland?"

"They survived the war, but he never saw them again."

May 9

Her room is dark, just the muted glow of the little TV I'm watching from across the room. She sleeps fitfully, then jerks awake.

"Rob?"

"Yeah, I'm right here. I've got the Clippers on."

Then the routine. First the TV goes off. Then the lamp switch on. The button that raises her head and back. The pillows. The hearing aid. A half glass of ginger ale and ice. She sips.

"Tell me about Grandma and Grandpa Ryder."

"They both came over from Norway. His name was Rytterager, but they changed it to Ryder."

"Thank God for that," I say.

"They met in a boarding house in Boston. She was playing the piano. They got married and moved to Brooklyn. She was very nice."

"Sigrid."

"Yes. But Grandpa Ryder could be very stern. He was an electrician and had very strong socialist beliefs. He was closely involved in union organizing, and very well read. He attended all the lectures at Cooper Union and he loved to makes his point."

"A blue collar intellectual."

"He really was."

"Dad used to say his father loved 'the people' but hated people."

"Well, not really. But he could be very disdainful. But also, he was the one who mounted the lights on the top of the Empire State Building. He was the real thing." She remembers. "Over the years he and I grew quite close."

Violet struggles to take another sip of ginger ale. I see the road ahead here, and it isn't pretty. She is slowly starving to death. But feeling no hunger and no pain. I plow on.

"And they had two sons, Dad and Uncle Bob."

"Yes, and Uncle Bob was the black sheep. He was an electrician too, and a communist. He would work on big projects for six months then travel the country, staying in YMCAs and writing. Always writing."

"And drinking whiskey."

"That too. At Grandpa's funeral, Grandma grew so angry at him when he showed up in a brown sweater and work pants!"

"Hey, do you remember at Grandma's funeral? Years later when Grandma died? It was just you, Dad, Uncle Bob, Annie and me. Remember?"

"And the minister."

"Yeah, it was some little chapel and there was a door on the side open to a courtyard. And a trickling fountain. And right in the middle of the minister's spiel Uncle Bob yelled out, 'Hey, is somebody taking a piss out there?!'"

Violet laughs. We laugh together. But suddenly she's flagging. I tuck her in, turn off the light, slip from the room, and step out into the cool night.

May 10

I show Violet this picture of my brothers with our Dad.

"Tell me about the '60s."

"Your father and I were so afraid for you boys because of Vietnam. The draft. When Paul graduated from Stanford he was called in to Hackensack for his physical but he failed because of his asthma. We were so relieved."

"And Ken?"

"Ken? Oh, boy. When he graduated from Colorado he joined the Peace Corps and went to Sierra Leone. But he was unhappy there and he came back to New Jersey. Dad was very upset. Ken talked of moving to Canada then decided to apply for conscientious objector status."

"And that's where the priests came in."

"Yes. I was friends with two anti-war priests who lived in the East Village. Father Jim and Father John."

"They must have known the Berrigan brothers."

"Oh, yes. They were all considered very radical at the time. Anyway, they helped Ken prepare his case as a conscientious objector. But suddenly the draft boards were tightening the restrictions for that. So Ken moved back to Colorado where he knew a sympathetic doctor and the doctor found some bone fragments in his ankle and that's how Ken got out. There were many doctors helping out like that."

"And I got number 140 in the ping pong ball lottery and that's how I stayed out."

"I remember," she says. "What a strange night. Watching those balls on television, each one a life."

"It was surreal. At Princeton, lots of us wore our numbers to class the next day. One of the guys walked into the lecture hall with #1 plastered to his shirt and we gave him a standing ovation."

We both grow lost in the memories. She speaks again, "That was a rotten war."

May 10

Violet's phone book. Tattered, frayed, overflowing with names, addresses, numbers, crossed-out numbers, new numbers, newer numbers. And sadly, many crossed out names. But she's alert now, time for Ken and me to pounce, because these periods are growing shorter and more precious between longer and longer naps.

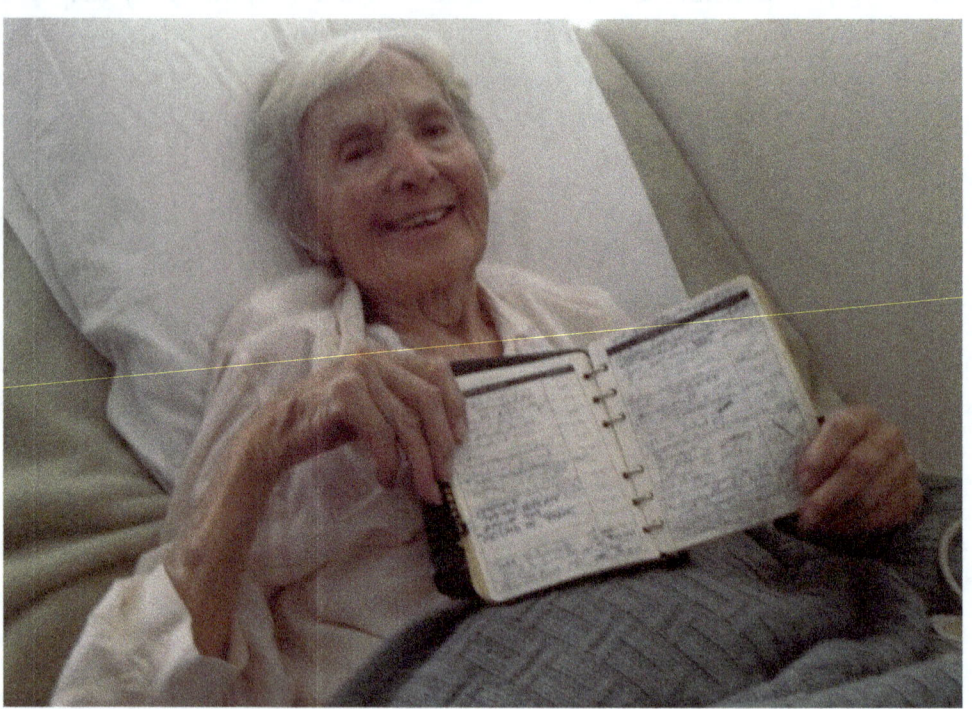

"Mom, who do you want to talk to today?"

"Your Aunt Sophia."

"Okay, I'll step out for a minute and try to reach her, then I'll hand you the phone."

This is our drill. I step out, reach Sophia back East and ask her a favor concerning her daughter Carolyn (our cousin). "Sophia, Violet has this wish that you and Carolyn reconcile your differences before she dies."

"Oh, jeez," says Sophia, who's 91 herself. "Robbie, I've tried and tried. Listen, dear, how about if I just fudge things a bit, okay? So she'll believe we're taking steps."

"That's all I'm asking. A little white lie. Just between you and me."

"And God," says Sophia.

So they have a short, heartfelt talk.

Violet with Aunt Sophia and Uncle Witold:

Then we work our way through the phone book: my cousin Karen, Violet's grandkids, including Hillary who's expecting Violet's second great-grandchild. Then an Ojai friend, Addie, then Violet's cousin's daughter, Gloria. (And by now Ken and I are looking at each other like, this could go on forever.) Violet ends each call with the same refrain: "Well, it was wonderful knowing you. I love you. Bye bye."

Then Violet reaches her dear old Afghan friend, Maga, in London, and they have a long talk. Violet is energized after she says goodbye: "What a woman she is."

"Tell us."

"Maga was born in Afghanistan and as a young girl was forced into an arranged marriage. They were Muslim. But Maga was very independent-minded and somehow she got out of the marriage and moved to England and ended up marrying Robert. She was tall and striking and he was very short and British, so when they got married, she wore her slippers. But he was a wonderful man and they had a good long marriage."

"Did she remain a Muslim?"

"Yes. And it's not so easy these days for good Muslims. In fact Robert became a Muslim too. Can you imagine his parents' reaction?"

"Uh, no."

"But that's what love will do."

Maga visiting Violet in California:

Violet rests her head back, half-closes her eyes. The tiredness comes suddenly now. With insistence. "One more call? How about Eleanor Hull in Boulder?"

"Yes, Eleanor. Although she may be dead. She turned 100 last year."

I scramble through the book and find her name. It hasn't been crossed out. I dial. A busy signal.

"It's busy, Mom."

"So maybe she's still alive."

"Maybe. Maybe she's talking to God. Making arrangements."

Violet smiles. "That's a nice thought."

And that fast she's asleep.

Saturday afternoon. Violet sleeps.

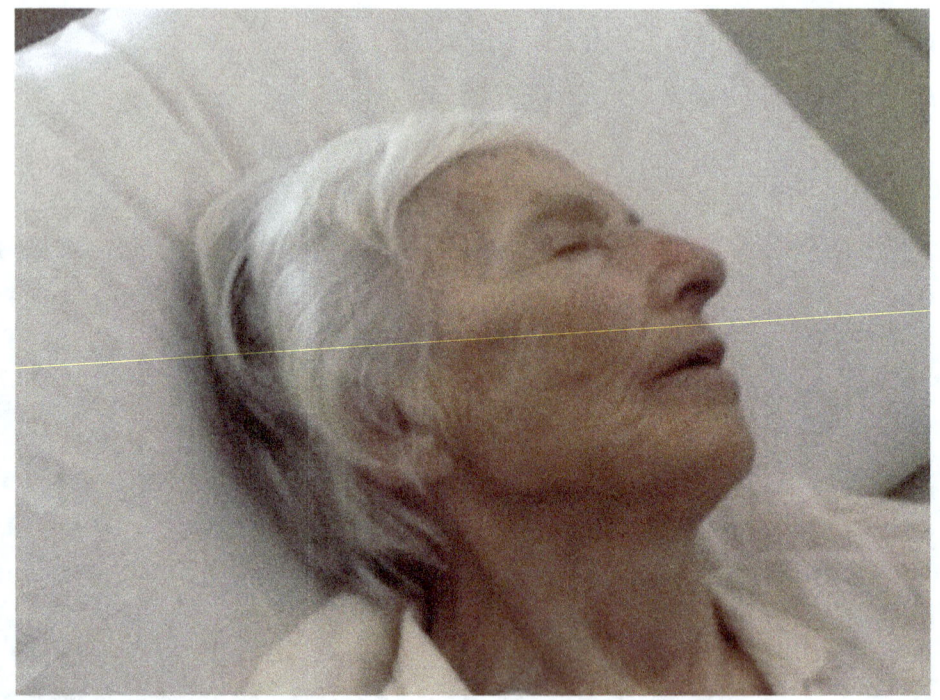

May 11

A beautiful, bittersweet Mother's Day. My brother Ken has to fly back to Bozeman this afternoon. Smiling through their tears… The weird thing is, Ken and his three kids in Montana have tickets to fly to California for a surf/climbing trip in just 10 days. He flew down quickly just to catch her alive. Now Ken says goodbye, not knowing what he'll find upon his return.

May 11

Somehow, some way, Violet gets up, grabs hold of her walker and makes it outside to sit in the sun. "Look how blue the sky is," she says. "And not a single cloud…"

"Mom, you know I've been putting some of these pictures and stories on Facebook."
"I know."
"And some of it, it's pretty intimate stuff. How you're facing your own death. And I want to make sure that's okay with you."
She thinks. "Everyone's so afraid of death. But there's no hiding from it. So yes, it's okay."
"Good. And when I take pictures, I'll make sure your hair looks nice."
"Forget the hair, just make sure I have my teeth in!"
We have a good laugh. Then she grows serious. "But Rob, you know the other part of my story, this is easy…what I'm going through…"
"Mom…"
"Compared to most. I see it everyday. All the medications, the surgeries. In and out of the hospital. The chronic pain that some people have. It's not always this easy."
"Okay," I say. "So I'll tell them you said that."
"Tell who?"
"The people who are following on Facebook."
"Oh. Good."

May 11

The twilight hour is the most difficult. The transition from sleeping to wakefulness for her last bathroom call has become slower and murkier. But once she's alert and has that sip of ginger ale, the stories tumble out.

"Tell me about your travels."

"Well, because your father worked for the United Nations, we lived and traveled all over Europe and the Middle East."

"Italy first," I say. "When we all lived there."

"Yes. But once you boys went away to college, then Dad and I really took off."

"Can you remember the cities? The capitals?"

"There was Rome, Paris, Warsaw, Oslo, London, Madrid, Cairo…there were a lot. Moscow, Istanbul, Jerusalem, Athens, Budapest… We stayed in all sorts of places, hotels mostly. Some were quite fancy and even had towel warmers in the bathroom, and some we were lucky to have a towel at all. Or even a bathroom."

She sips and thinks.

"Your father had several dangerous assignments over the years. First was the Belgian Congo. That was bad. I didn't go there. But then in the Gaza Strip and Southern Lebanon. We lived in an apartment in Haifa for those. He was most concerned about the road mines. But he never got hurt. Sometimes when he was very busy, I would go traveling by myself. Or sometimes Aunt Rosalie would come over and we would travel together. We had so much fun. We were sisters, but we were also best friends."

"Did any men ever try to pick you up? You and Rosalie?"

She thinks. Then smiles.

"No, but one time with Lee DiMarco, it was in Livorno. In Italy. And Lee was driving and you remember how much fun she was…we were stopped at a light, and a big truck pulled up, filled with Italian men, and they started flirting with us. So Lee stuck her head out the window and smiled at them and suddenly crossed her eyes, and her eyes could really cross, and that stopped them in their tracks. While they were all laughing, Lee floored it and that was the end of that."

May 12

Violet asks if I can phone Paul's daughter, Jane in Montana, so she can say goodbye. I dial and reach her and say, "Hey, Jane are you in Bozeman?"

"I'm actually fly-fishing in Wyoming."

"What river are you on?"

"The North Platte."

"How is it?"

"The fishing's great, but the weather sucks."

I tell Jane that Violet can only stay on for a minute. I hand over the phone, and Violet speaks to her with much love, then whispers goodbye. I take the phone back.

"Jane?"

Jane in a happier time

A gasp, a sob. "Oh, Rob…"

"It's okay. She's doing it right. It's okay."

We talk for a minute, then say goodbye and hang up.

Jane, crying in the rain along the banks of the North Platte.

May 12

The hospice nurse and social worker come visit Violet. Her toes are turning red and her heels are cracking, so Nurse Stephanie builds her a pillow tent to protect them. I tell them the story from last November when Violet fell and went into the hospital. We thought she might be dying, so I asked her, "Mom, you've been around so long, you've experienced so much, what advice do you have for the rest of us?" (I was expecting some great spiritual insight.)

   Her answer: "Take care of your teeth and your feet."

Stephanie and Jennifer

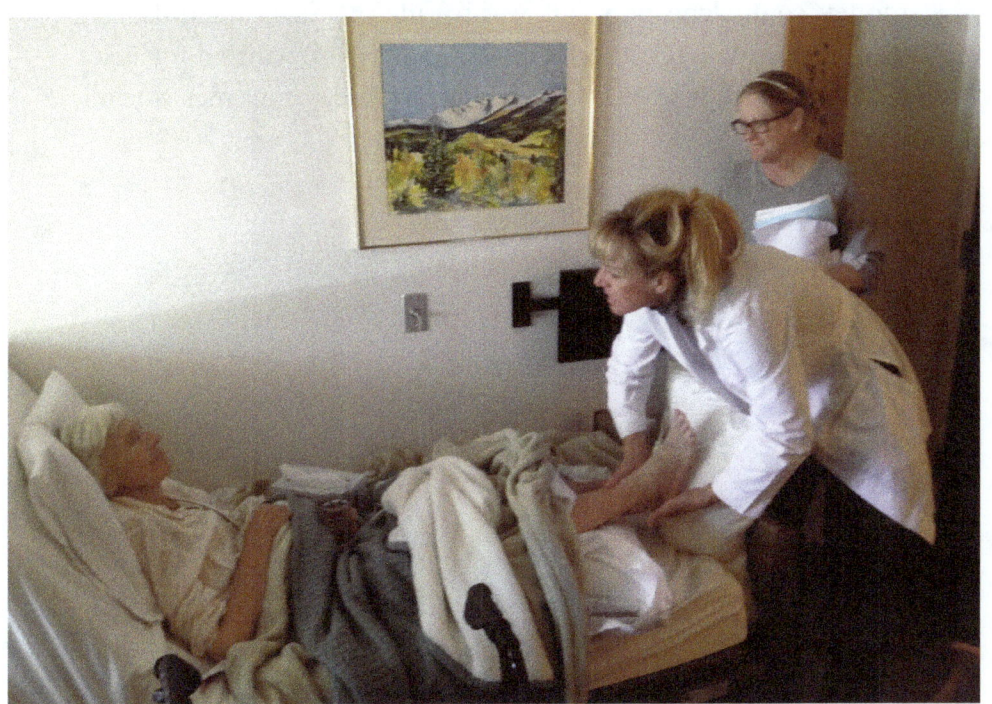

May 12

"When we were dating, Dad and I loved to go dancing. There were dance halls all over Brooklyn. And sometimes we even went to the jazz clubs in Manhattan. But we didn't have much money, so our cheapest date was to ride the Staten Island Ferry. You could ride back and forth as much as you wanted for just a nickel. Once we started kissing, we would sometimes ride all afternoon and into the night."

May 13

Violet is weaker this morning. Disoriented. She keeps asking what day it is. But when I ask for more travel stories, she grows clear. Her gaze is more fixed now, and her eyes narrower, as she travels back in time.

"After your father retired for the second time" (he'd been called back to help with the Cyprus Conflict) "we moved into the house you boys built us in Colorado. We loved the aspen trees, how they shimmered in the breeze. And all the mountain flowers. Columbine was my favorite. But after a few years, the elevation was too hard on Dad's heart."

"Gold Hill is over 8,000 feet," I say. "We weren't thinking about that at the time…"

"But those years meant so much to us. Anyway, we moved to Ventura with the view of the ocean and that was nice. But we realized we didn't really know North America that well. So one summer we drove up the California coast and all across Canada. We camped every night, with our sleeping bags and little tent. It was beautiful. Then we drove down the East Coast, visiting friends and family. From Maine to Florida. Then back to Ventura."

"That's a lot of miles."

"We loved it. We traveled very well together. Then that winter we decided to explore Baja. So we drove down, thinking we'd treat ourselves by staying in nice hotels."

"Hey, you deserved some creature comforts. You were both in your sixties right?"

"Oh, yes. But the beaches were so beautiful we hated to leave them at night. We didn't have our camping gear so we bought two thick Mexican blankets…they were very colorful…and we slept on the beach at night, under those huts."

"Palapas. With the thatched roofs and open sides."

"Yes. All day, we would walk the beach and read and swim. Dad would spend hours in the warm water. You remember what a wonderful swimmer he was. Then in the late afternoon we would dig for scallops and clams, and luckily we had brought along the hibachi."

"The heavy one, with the wood handles."

"And every evening we would eat grilled scallops and clams with limes and tequila…"

May 13

Paul's second daughter Hillary just sent this picture from Seattle.

"Look, Mom, it's Hillary and Charlotte. And the baby's due June 5th."

I hold out my phone. Violet reaches and touches Hillary's belly on the small screen.

"It's a boy," I say.

"I know," she whispers. "Paul will teach him to fly fish."

May 13

A quiet evening.

"You look beautiful in this light. Let me take your picture."

"Okay." She smiles.

"Mom, you're always smiling. People are gonna think there's nothing wrong with you. They'll think we're pulling a fast one."

"Okay, how's this?"

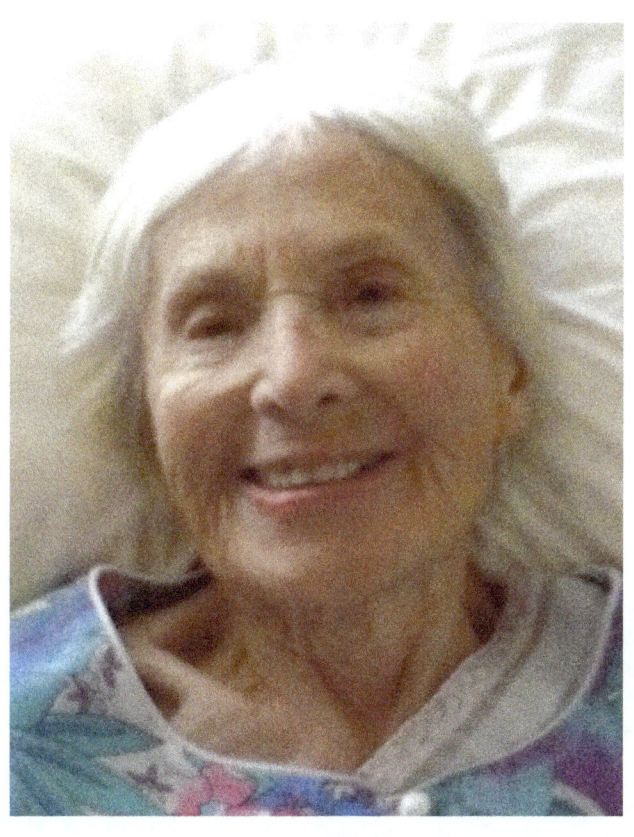

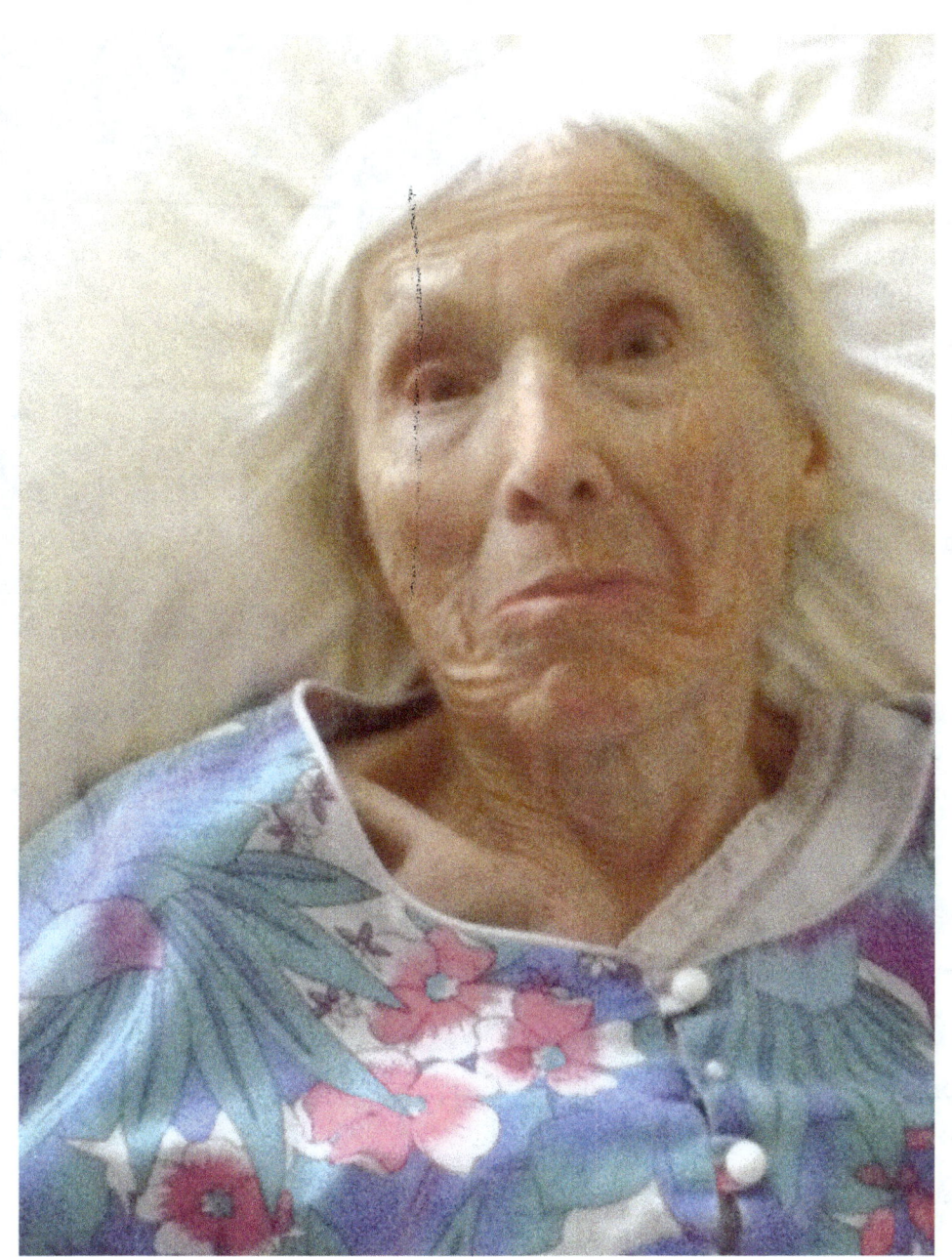

May 13

It's a hot night in Ojai. The Santa Anas have been gusting, erratic. Then suddenly vanishing at sunset, leaving a dead calm. The moon high and white in the black sky, shrouded by a lone cloud. Red flag warnings. Wildfires in San Diego County and Lompoc. On a night like this, in the crackling dry air, just a whiff of smoke will raise the hairs on your neck. They're predicting a three-day extreme heat and wind event.

As I drive the few short blocks to Violet's care facility, I think, maybe this is her time. Maybe she'll go out in a hot biblical blast. But I remember the hospice nurse's caution: "The dying can live for days, even weeks, without food. Even without water. It happens."

I find her awake in the cool dark room, air-conditioner humming. I turn on the lamp and help her get comfortable. A quiet resignation has set in her eyes. This is new.

"So, Mom, you've thought about your death…"
"Oh, yes."
"And it's okay to talk about it?"

"Yes." Her voice gains strength. "Sure."

"Do you think of your afterlife? I mean, do you think you'll retain some sort of consciousness after you die? A sense of self?"

"There's no way of really knowing, is there, until it happens."

"It's the one great mystery, I guess."

She works to gather her thoughts. Finally: "A sense of self seems less important as I grow closer. But sometimes I feel very strongly that my spirit, my soul, will merge with the other souls. It's just a feeling. But it feels true. And simple."

"You know what Ken says? He thinks you'll return to Earth as a Bodhisattva."

"What's that?"

"It's a Buddhist belief. Maybe he picked it up from his time in Bhutan. Enlightened souls, when they die, are offered a conscious choice to remain in a place of enlightenment or to return to Earth to help others and to share their wisdom."

She smiles weakly.

"Well, I don't know about that. I'd have to get some rest first."

May 14

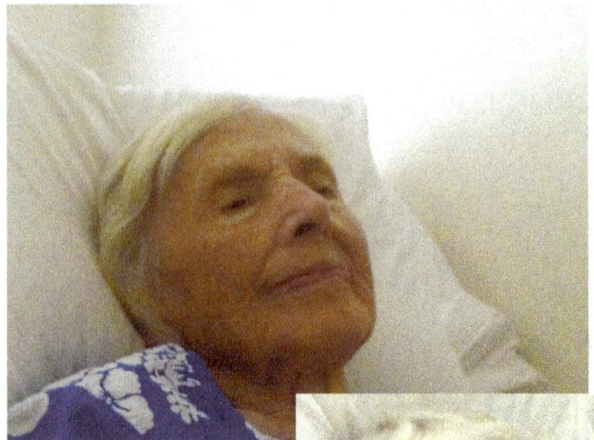

Wednesday morning. Violet is slow to awaken. A sprig of jasmine to greet another day in this life.

May 14

101 degrees. Winds swirling. Much worse elsewhere in the Southland. Fires burning in Carlsbad, Rancho Cucamonga, Camp Pendleton, Cal State San Marcos, Pacific Palisades… all over the place. More than 20 homes lost so far. They're saying hotter tomorrow.

Violet is quiet today, so we sit in the cool of her room and watch the fire news. I have a strong sense that she isn't ready to check out in the midst of this biblical blast. It's not her style anyway. She's hit a steady rhythm here and this heat wave too shall pass.

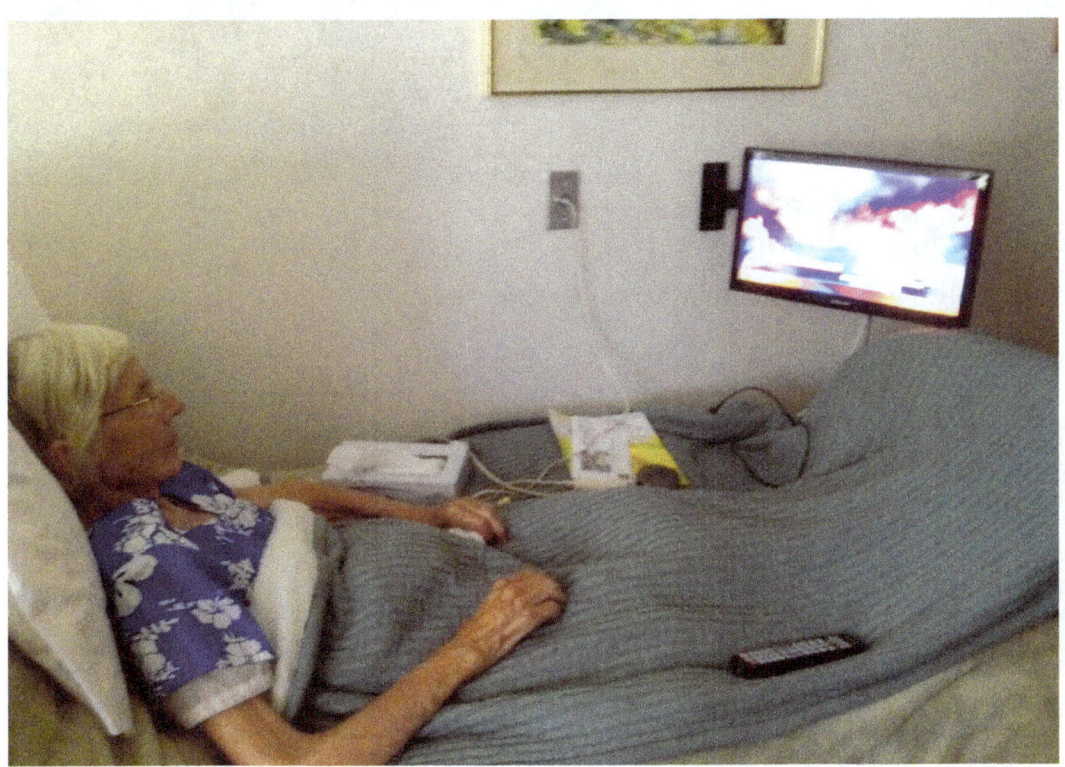

May 15

Another blistering day in Ojai. Violet recalls the cool blue summers on Lake George.

"We would leave the day after you kids got out of school and not come back until Labor Day. All summer. Except for your father who had to work. But he came up on weekends and for two weeks in August."

"How did you pack all that camping gear in one car?"

"Well, we had the little trailer too."

"Yeah, the trailer with one wheel. I never understood why it didn't tip over."

"And your father always tested the boat motor before we left."

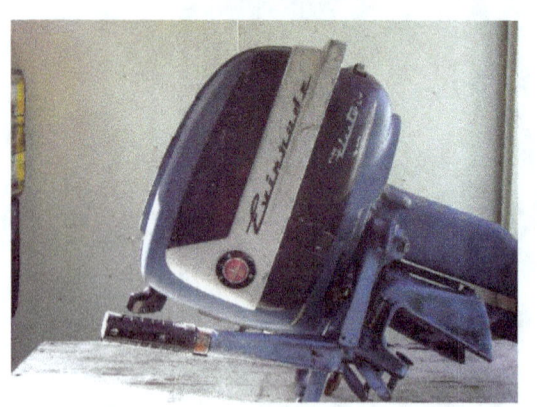

"It was an old Evinrude. I remember him filling up a big trash can with the hose in the backyard, then mounting it with the propeller in the water."

Violet's eyes fill with light. "All the neighborhood kids would come to watch. Joey Sireno, Pauley Kuhn, Erica Friedman…

"He would yank and yank, and it always started with a racket and a cloud of blue smoke and there'd be water flying everywhere. All us kids would jump back and Dad would look at us and yell, 'How do I get to Norway?!'"

May 15

Violet's fallen back asleep. I call Stephanie, the hospice nurse.

"My Mom loved the foot massage you gave her yesterday."

"Oh, I was just loving her up a bit. She's so darn lovable."

"She seems okay today. Peaceful."

"Yeah, but I did notice a decline from the day before."

"I know," I say.

"She's not resisting, but she's not giving in either."

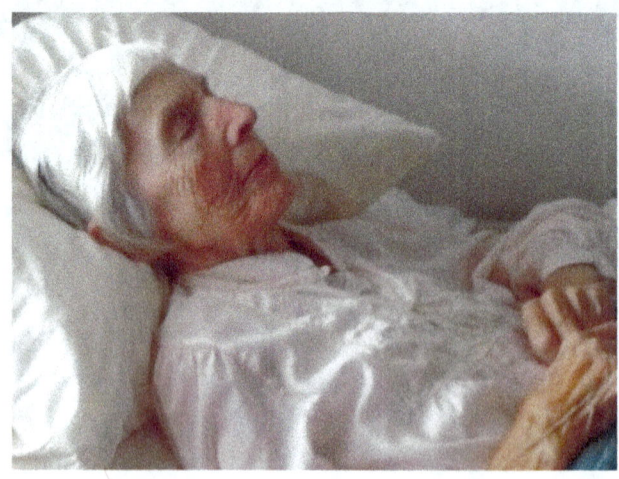

May 15

When she wakes, Violet is right back to Lake George. (It's in the Adirondacks, the summer home of Georgia O'Keefe for many years.)

"It was a five-hour drive up Route 17, but you kids never squabbled on the way to the lake."

"Not like we did on the way to Aunt Sophie's on Staten Island for Sunday dinner."

"When we reached Bolton Landing, I would shop for groceries while Dad and you boys would unload the car at the boat docks."

"F.R. Smith & Sons. And we'd rent an aluminum row boat, and Dad would mount the motor on it."

"We always camped on Turtle Island, Campsite 1, right on the point. And Aunt Rosalie and Uncle Joe and Karen would have Campsite 2, and sometimes your cousin Carolyn would join us."

"It was pretty primitive, wasn't it? I mean, that's a long summer without plumbing or electricity."

"We did fine. Each site had a picnic table and a stone fireplace with a heavy grill. Plus we had a four-burner Coleman stove. And two ice chests. Every week the ice boat would come around and deliver big blocks of ice."

"Just like in Brooklyn."

She smiles and lapses into silence.

"So you cooked outside all summer long."

"We made everything. Chicken, mashed potatoes, blueberry pancakes with wild blueberries you kids would pick. And once Rosalie and I even made a pot roast."

"Mark camped with us one summer."

"He loved it."

"It wasn't hard, with a baby like that?"

"Not especially. But he loved playing in the fireplace, and I was worried there might be a hot coal…but there never was. He'd be covered in ashes."

"Yeah, but, Mom, there's something you're leaving out here."

"What?"

"The outhouse."

She laughs.

"We all hated that thing. The smell. And the spiders. Aunt Rosalie especially."

"What about Dad and the glove?"

"Oh, that was a night. We were playing Scrabble at the table with two lanterns burning."

(Old Colemans, their fragile mantles throwing a harsh white light.)

"Aunt Rose had to go to the outhouse. All you kids were in your tents already. She took a flashlight and off she went. And your father found one of my green rubber dishwashing gloves and put it on and crept off after her."

"There was a crescent moon carved in the outhouse door."

"Yes. And poor Rosalie was sitting in there when suddenly this green hand came reaching in through the hole. She screamed so loud I think she woke up all of Turtle Island!"

"Was she angry?"

"Oh, boy. But Uncle Joe got a real kick out of it."

The memories carry energy for her. She's out of time, reliving the past.

May 15

"As long as I knew him, your father loved the water, and he loved to row. When he drove up to Lake George on weekends, sometimes I could see the stress from his job at the UN and I knew to leave him alone. He'd take the boat out by himself and go for a long row, and when he got back to the island, he'd be happy and ready to talk."

"I remember the Fourth of July," I say. "We'd all go out to the point and watch for the fireworks in Lake George Village."

"And you boys made your own. I would save those big juice cans, and you'd punch holes in them and string them with long wire handles."

"I remember that. We'd fill them with hot coals from the fireplace."

"It was so dangerous, I don't think kids would be allowed to do that today. But you carried them out to the point, it was pitch black, and you'd swing them in big circles and the sparks would fly everywhere."

May 15

Thursday afternoon. Violet wakes up groggy.

"What day is it?"

"Thursday."

"What time is it?"

"Five o'clock."

"In the morning?"

"Afternoon."

"Oh."

"Mom, you know who's coming from Montana tomorrow, right? Adam and the girls. Ken's kids. Your grandkids. And you get to meet Adam's wife, Julia."

I show her their pictures on my phone.

"Here's Adam and Julia at their wedding. And Lindsay rock climbing. And here's Genevieve cross-country skiing with Adam."

"And they're coming tomorrow?"

"Yeah, with Ken too. But, Mom, if you need to let go…they'll understand. Okay?"

"Yes. I guess I've said goodbye to everyone already. We'll just see what happens."

"Okay. I'll be back later tonight. Around nine o'clock. There's something I want to ask you."

May 15

The sky is dark. The lamp is low. Violet wakes from her evening nap. Her eyes are perfectly clear and she's smiling.

"Rob?"
"Yeah, I'm here."
"I just had the nicest dream. I dreamt that I had already died and everything was in place. It was so peaceful…"
"Wow. Where were you? Do you remember a specific place in your dream?"
"It wasn't like that. It wasn't like anything we know."
"What was it then?"
"Just complete calm. Everything was in place."

I see her slip back into the dream. Her face fills with bliss. A minute passes, and she opens her eyes again.

"But, Mom, you didn't die. You're here still. How does it feel to wake up?"
"Well, I guess it's easier now that I know where I'm going…"
"Here, let's sit you up. And please, let the bed do the work."

I push the up button for the backrest. As it slowly rises, she once again beats it to the punch, her stomach muscles an easy match for her frail upper body. The backrest finally joins her. I hand her a glass of ginger ale on ice and she sips.

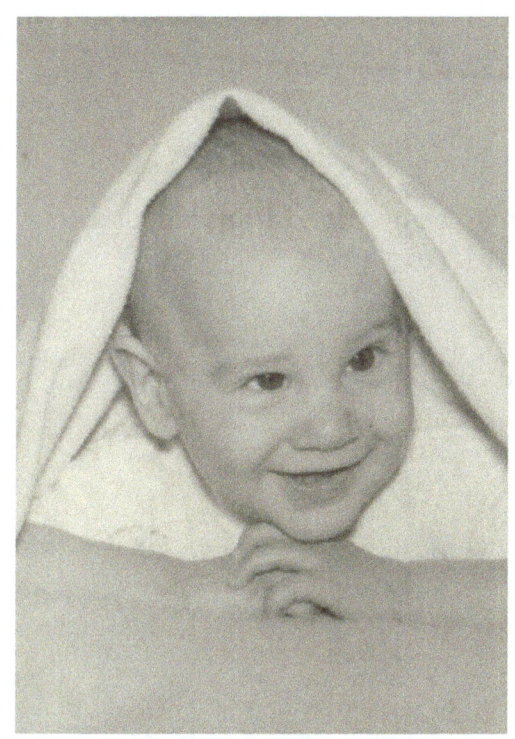

"You wanted to ask me something."

"Yes. Mom, you were raised Catholic. And I always felt that you had a deep faith in God. Not just the church, but between you and God. That you were deeply connected."

"Yes."

"So let me ask you…when Mark died, did that make you question your faith?"

She smiles as if I just asked the dumbest question in the world.

"Oh, no. I was grateful for the time Mark was with us."

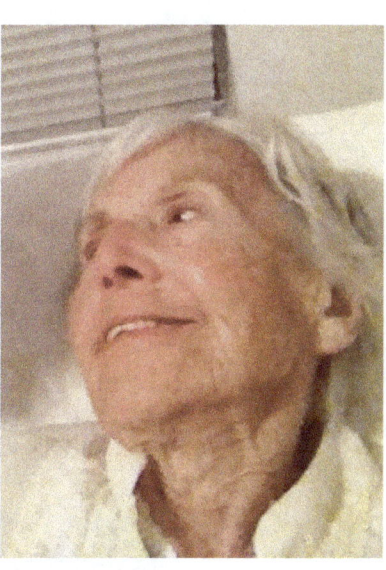

"You weren't angry at Him? That God could just let Mark die like that? He was what, 18-months-old, and that God could just take him away from us? And you never once blamed Him."

"No. We can't blame God for what we lose. We can only be grateful for what He has given us."

She considers her words.

"To have faith is to have gratitude. Mark was God's gift to us."

May 16

When the phone rings at 2 a.m. this morning, I think okay, this is it. But it isn't The Gables calling, it's Violet, wondering what day it is. Jeez.

And here we are a few hours later, my ex Andrea curling her hair again. The grandkids are coming from Montana tonight. Will they get here in time? Piece of cake.

What good is a ticking clock for Violet's story if she keeps rewinding it?

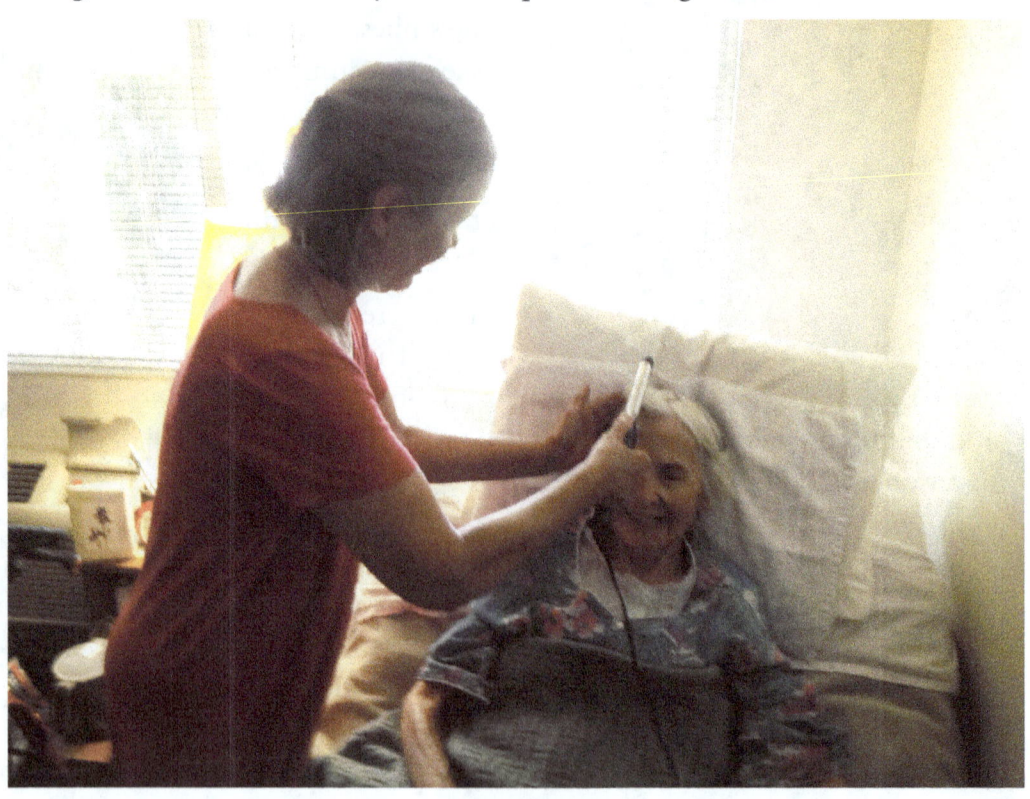

May 16

Violet's quite proud of her Jitterbug cell phone, but it might be time to "disappear" it (between my 2 a.m. wake-up call and now this):

"Mom, Stephanie from hospice told me that you called over there today. That you wanted to cancel your memorial service Sunday."

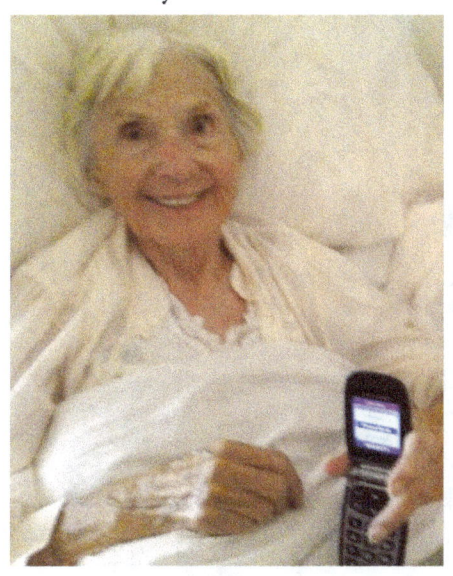

"Did they cancel it?"

"Mom, no one ever scheduled it. We're not gonna schedule any services until you die, right?"

"That's why you should cancel it."

"Or here's an idea, maybe we should just have it. That way you could be there too. See who shows up."

I see her wheels turning. Oh, man, what did I just say?

"Mom, I'm joking. There's no service Sunday."

"I'm very disoriented."

"I know. You're getting a little loopy."

She stares at me.

"In a good way, I mean. Things are getting confusing, but you seem nice and, uh, relaxed about it?"

She continues staring.

"Hey, I heard from Ken. He and the kids landed at LAX."

"I better get some rest."

"You and me both."

May 16

Oh, the tears are flowing in Ojai tonight.

Lindsay and Genevieve turning on the love.

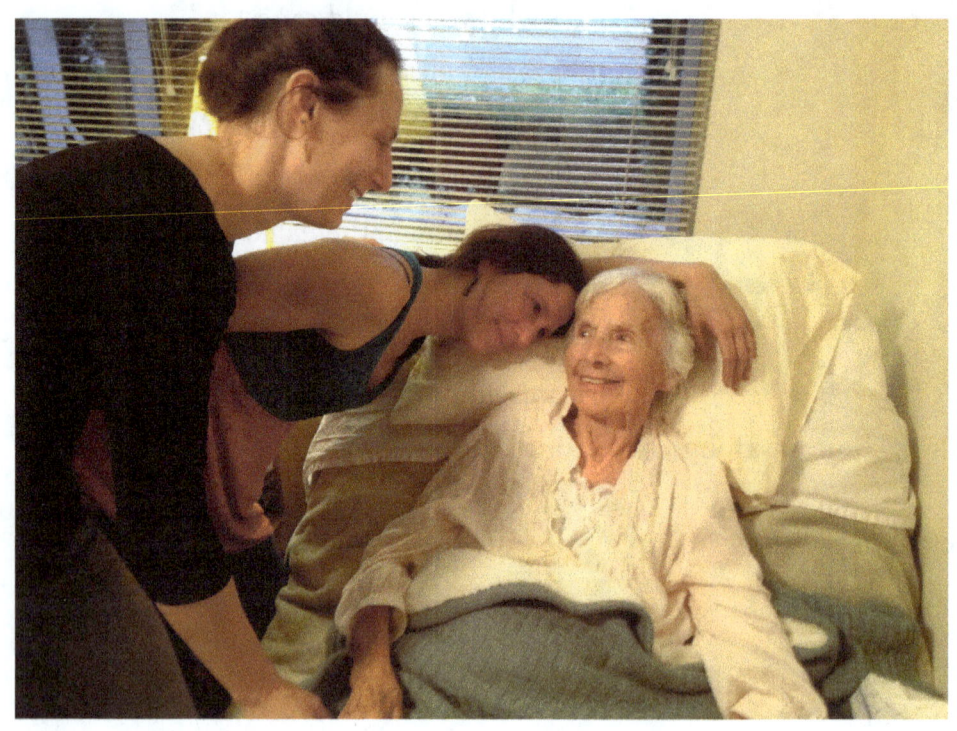

Adam introducing his bride, Julia.

Violet touching Julia's face.

   "Adam says you're a nurse."

   "Yes."

   "You must be a wonderful nurse."

May 17

Violet's exhausted. She spends all day Saturday sleeping, her frail body contorted at times, as if saying, okay, enough already. But by now, well into Saturday night, she's relaxed. And the strain has left her face.

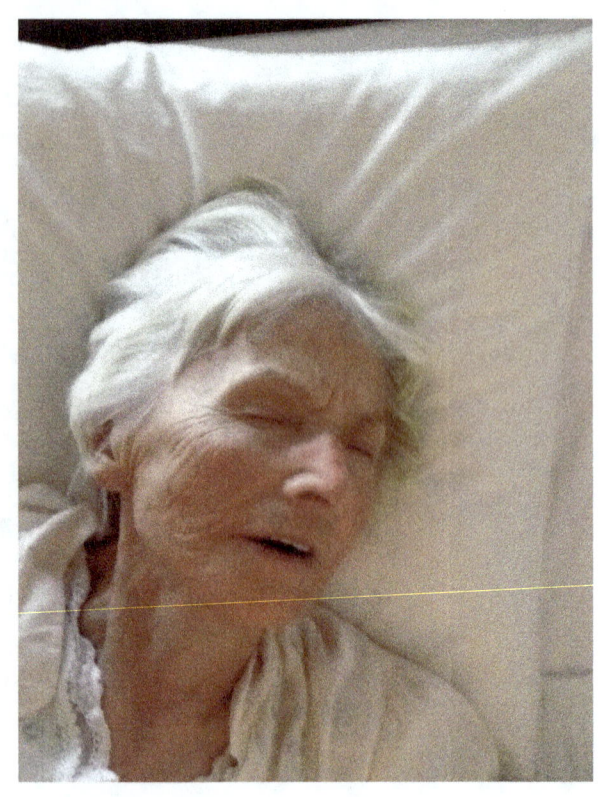

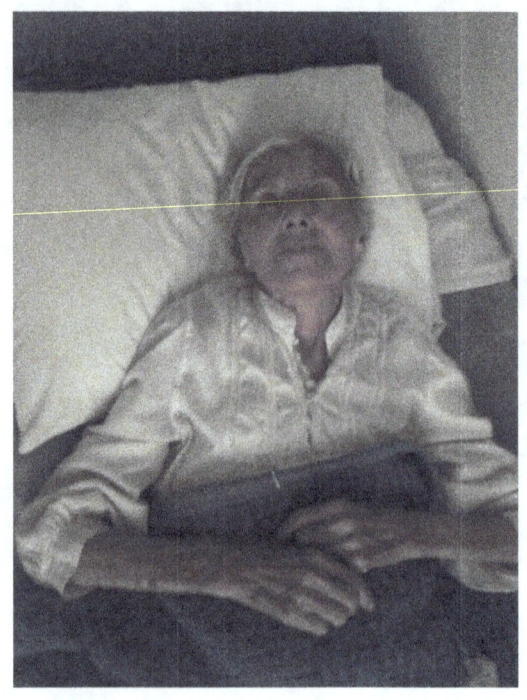

It was well worth the effort, holding out to see Adam, Genevieve and Lindsay. Plus finally meeting her grand daughter-in-law, Julia. Energy well spent. The circle has been completed. She's at peace.

We'll see what Sunday morning brings.

May 18

Sunday morning. Violet awakens to receive Holy Communion from the wonderful Helen. These two have known each other for many years from out at St. Joseph's.

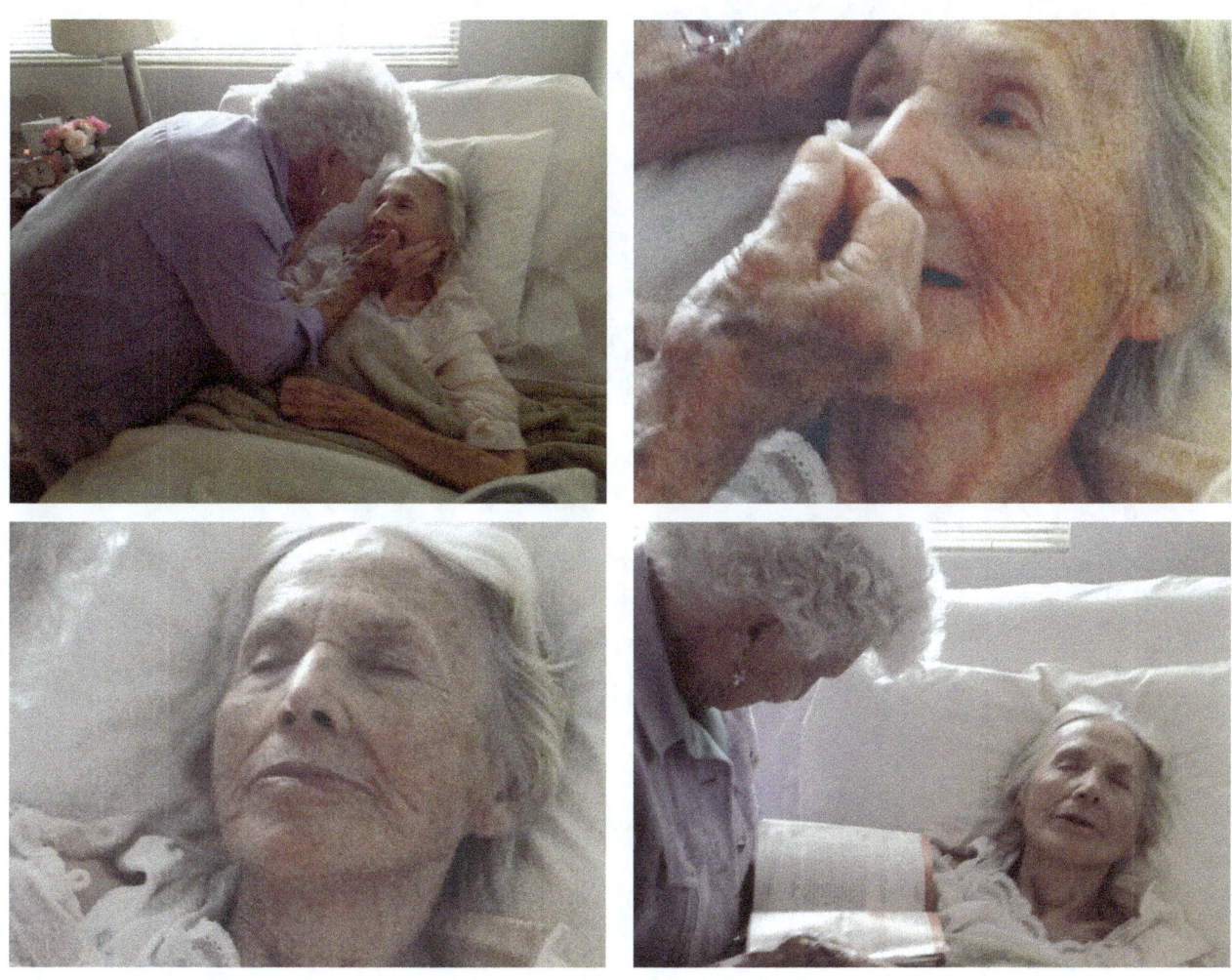

Sunday afternoon. After a morning visit, the Montanans are off surfing.

I peruse Violet's bookshelf as she sleeps. Tucked into her bible, these old photographs. First, Violet's Polish parents being married in Brooklyn. Monica Mitunewitz was 16, her new husband, Anthony Lyczkowski, 17. The following year our Aunt Rosalie was born. And Violet the year after that, 1918. The second photograph, the two sisters at their First Holy Communion.

May 19

Monday morning. Violet weakens. She'll be telling no more stories. Her hearing aids remain in their small round box. Her glasses go unused. She is in no pain, but even the smallest sip of water causes her to gag. Her organs have begun to fail. She mostly sleeps.

Any more pictures of her will be from the past.

During her few waking moments, her mind is remarkably clear. I show her this pic of her grandkids, taken just last night. She touches it and smiles.

May 20

Hold the presses! Put away that tissue box! And okay, I lied yesterday when I said I'd be posting no more current pictures. Because when I arrive this morning, Violet is sitting up, clear-eyed and smiling. She asks to smell the roses that the grandkids brought her Sunday.

What is going on here? It's as if her senses are growing more acute, her appreciation of the smallest moments deepening. I think we were all expecting she'd slowly slip into a misty twilight and then go gentle into that good night. Instead, this burst of adrenalin.

She asks what the grandkids are doing today. I tell her, the Montana gang—rock-climbing in Sespe Gorge. And Andre? He's in school, then working on the farm. And how's his knee? Beginning to heal. She smiles and says good, and that fast, she's asleep.

I catch Rosa and Maria in the hallway and tell them about the roses.

"Oh, that nothing," says Rosa. "Early this morning, she press the button and you know what she want? She want to see menu!"

"What?!"

"It's true," says Maria. "So we brought her a piece of toast and coffee."

"And then she ask for jelly! And she eat the whole thing!"

"Without throwing up?"

"Without throwing up."

"I love your Mom," says Rosa.

"I love her too," says Maria.

May 20

Violet volunteered all her life. She loved to tutor children, and they loved her in return. My father called her the saint. She hated that and would give him a look.

And once in a blue moon, her temper would really flare. My Dad would give us boys a heads up, whispering, "Here comes the hurricane," and we'd suddenly become engrossed in our homework.

May 20

Another minor miracle today. It seems that caregiver Christine was born in Poland and spent her childhood there before being adopted by a family in Ventura.

"Wyglądasz pięknie dziś," says Christine. (You look beautiful today.)

"Wyglądasz pięknie każdego dnia," says Violet. (You look beautiful every day.)

And get this, they share the same birthday, August 6th! Violet, 1918, Christine, 1980.

Footnote: Shortly after posting this, I got a message on FB from Christine - "Wow Rob....I can't believe you got a picture of her touching my face!!!!...she has such a tender touch!!! Her hands were so soft and I don't think there was any part of her palm that wasn't touching my cheek. I teared up....it was intense....residents don't touch caregivers like that."

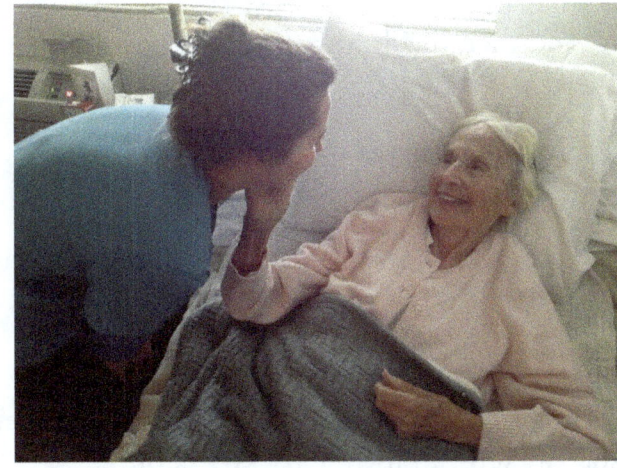

May 21

Wednesday morning. It looks like yesterday's buoyancy was Violet's last hurrah. The hospice literature mentions it, "A sudden surge of energy. A temporary increase in appetite."

She's sleeping, her breathing shallow, her feet and hands cooler to the touch. Suddenly her arms start flailing, fingers tugging at her nightgown. Stephanie the hospice nurse arrives and I ask about it.

"It's called terminal agitation. If it grows severe we can give her some Atavan."

Stephanie inspects Violet's feet, pointing out how the soles have grown ashen.

"This is called mottling. And fluid will start collecting in her lungs. She'll start coughing some."

"And then the death rattle."

"That's what causes it. The fluid. But she's a way away."

"She cut off her diaper last night," I say.

"What?"

"Yeah, somehow she reached for her little scissors and cut it off and pushed it down by her feet. She said it was uncomfortable."

"She is something else."

Stephanie leaves, saying she'll be back this afternoon. So I sit, holding Violet's hand. Finally, she awakens. I raise the backrest a bit.

"I had a nice dream," she whispers.

"Tell me."

"It was your father and me, at Stanford (my brother Paul's alma mater). They gave us snacks."

"That sounds nice."

A long silence.

"I'm drifting away," she says.

"I know. But it's sweet, right? A sweet way to go."

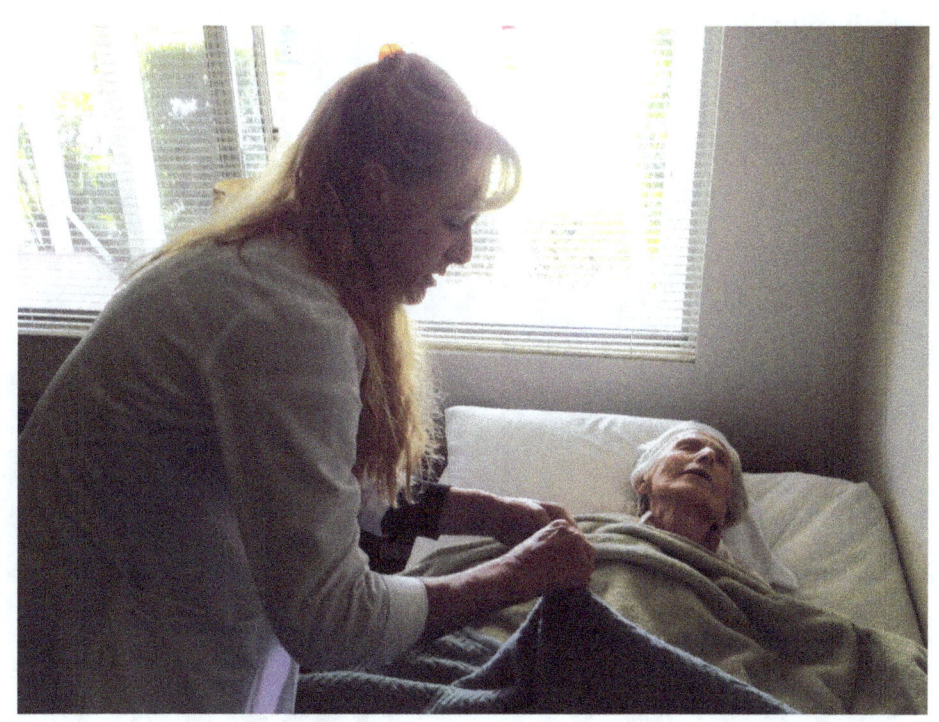

May 21

Wednesday, 2 p.m. Violet sleeps as Constance from hospice rubs her feet. Another caregiver with the perfect blend of the loving and the practical.

I ask her, "How long do you think?"

She considers.

"From the time I spent with your Mom, she'll need to know that everything is in order before she allows herself to go."

"It is. Bills, the mortuary, her service, stuff for Goodwill and Help of Ojai. The trust. Everything is buttoned up."

"Make sure you tell her that."

"I already have."

"Tell her again."

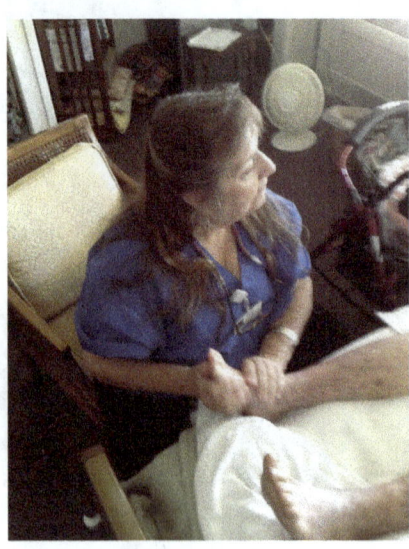 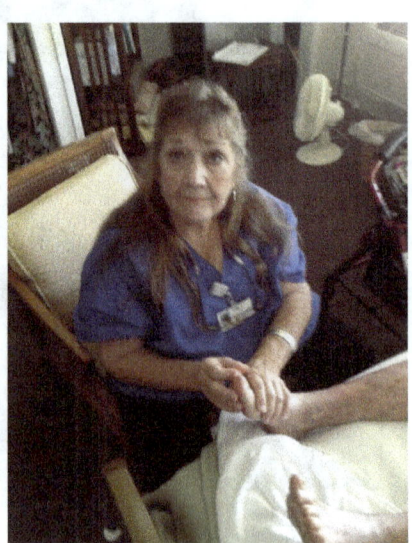

Wednesday, late afternoon. Violet perks up when Ken and the grandkids stop by. I take a few pictures. Violet has become quite good at taking direction these past few weeks.

"Good," I say. "Now Ken, Mom, look at each other. Man, I hate this backlight. Lemme get tighter. Okay, now look at the camera. Nice. Sweet."

Ken says, "Rob the director."

Violet, haltingly, "You should be paying us a salary."

Wednesday, 6 p.m. An unexpected sun shower. A modest rainbow crosses the bluffs. I post this pic and a Chinese friend comments, "Violet is the highest color in the rainbow, the highest wavelength. And in Buddhism, violet represents the crown chakra, the chakra of enlightenment."

Okay. So maybe this is the sign we've been waiting for. Maybe tonight is the night.

Or maybe not.

Wednesday night. Violet sleeps fitfully—out of rhythm. Her body is tragically thin now, while somehow her face…that face. Finally, she stirs and half opens her eyes. Struggling to say something. I lean forward: "Tell me."

Then, very slowly: "I had a dream. I was standing in the parking lot of Suzanne's and I didn't have a ride home. Somebody said they would call a taxi, and I said I don't know, it's quite far. Then someone else said, it's free, so I said okay. Then they decided that everyone would have a free ride home."

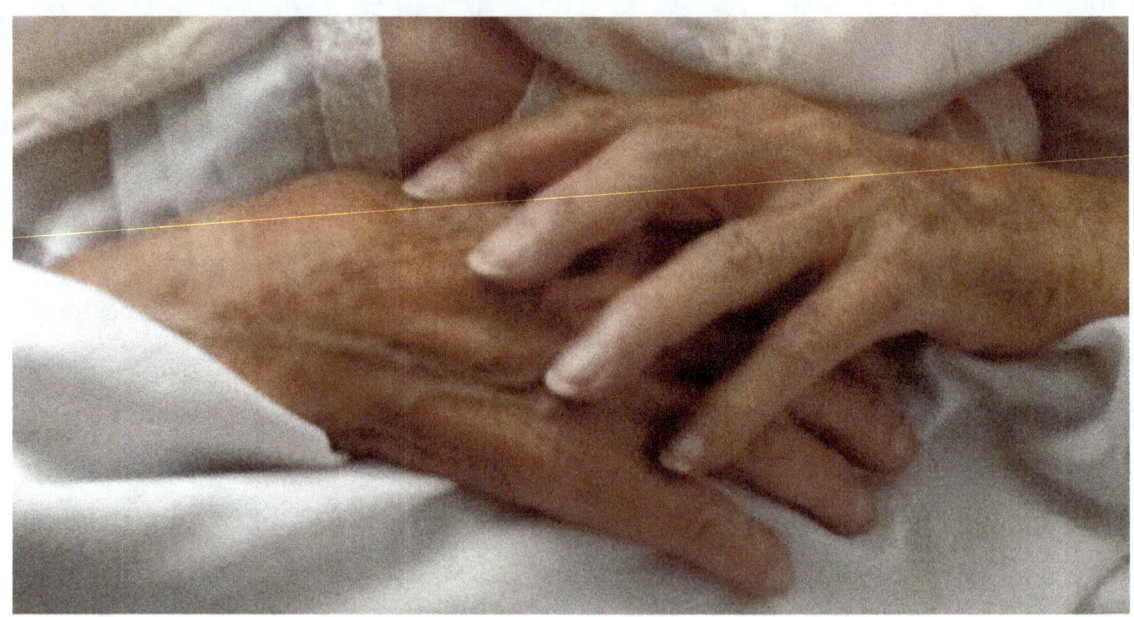

May 22

I receive a message from my dear childhood friend from Italy, Tony DiMarco. His wonderful dad Joe, worked for the United Nations too, and his mom Lee, was Violet's closest friend. The DiMarcos all ended up back in the states. Tony's been following on Facebook.

"Robbie, I have read every one of your stories about your mom…it's like reading chapters in a book…and I don't want it to end….the last time I saw your mother she came to River Edge to visit my parents…my mom called me and made sure I came down to see her…my mom made a 10 course Italian meal and we spent all day telling stories about the UN and Camp Darby… then your mom asked me for a favor….would I drive her to a cemetery about a half hour away to visit your brother's grave…it took us about an hour to find it off RT 17…when she saw how big the cemetery had expanded she got nervous…we drove around in it and then suddenly she saw a huge tree…..she directed me to it…in about 5 minutes she found the stone….she took out of her purse a small hand shovel and dug a few inches into the dirt…your father had just passed away and she wanted to bury some of his ashes with your brother…we both were crying…I will never forget that moment…prayers and thoughts are with you, Ken, Paul and your families…we all know the ending to this story…but I want the chapters to continue…"

May 22

The grandkids sit vigil. Violet stirs occasionally. Manages a smile. A touch. Always reaching to touch a face…

Thursday 10 p.m. Violet sleeps.

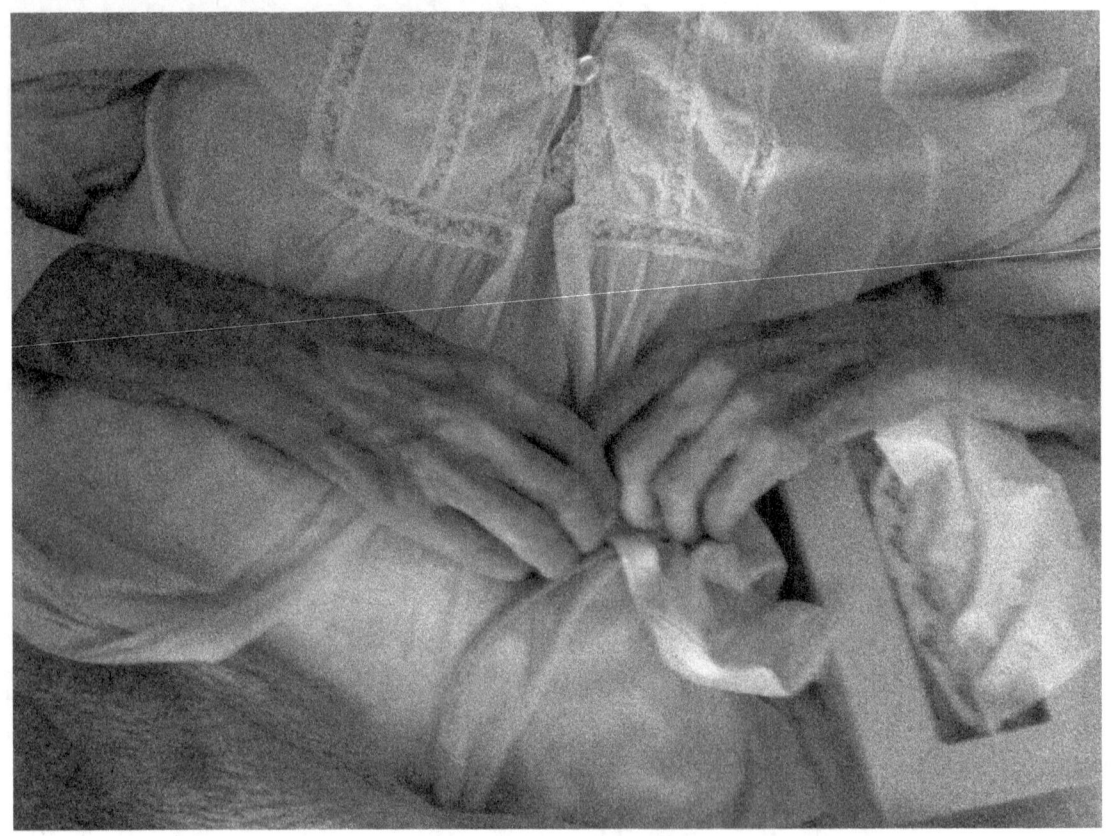

May 23

Friday. Violet sleeps. My Dad and little brother Mark wait patiently.

May 24

A cool grey morning
The Montanans say goodbye
Heart rocks on the beach

May 25

Sunday morning. Violet wakes up, eyes glassy, voice hoarse. She's so close to death now—skin pale and mottled, hair tufting, hands cool to the touch.

"Am I in Gold Hill?"

"No, Mom, you're in Ojai. You're still alive."

"What?"

"You're still alive!"

I'm speaking so loudly the whole place must hear me.

"Oh. What day is it?"

"Sunday."

"Communion?"

"Yes, Helen is coming."

Violet waits in silence. I slip out and spot Helen in the hall.

"Can you see Violet first?"

"Of course."

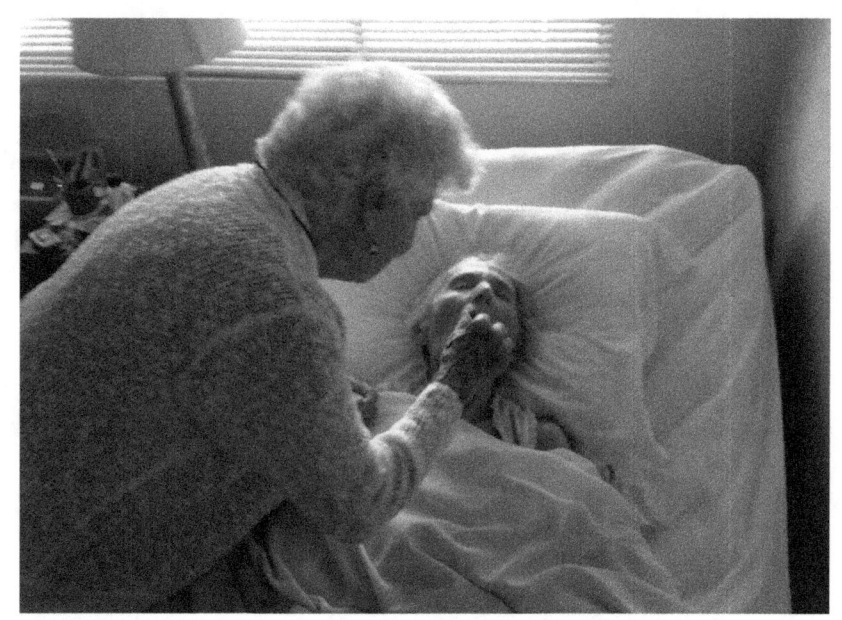

As we enter her room, Violet immediately throws open her mouth—a hatchling craning for sustenance. Helen quickly breaks off a small piece of wafer and places it on her tongue. A short prayer, a kiss to the forehead. Violet sinks back into her pillow and closes her eyes.

Sunday, late night. Violet is agitated. Gasping for breath. Hands tangling in her bedclothes, tugging at her sheet and blanket. Reaching. Eyes half-open, glazed over. Muttering, unintelligible. I take her hands, cross them in her lap and hold them there. She finally calms. I lean over her and kiss her.

"Mom, it's time for you to go now. It's time. God is there for you. And Dad. And Mark. Mark's there too. Waiting for you. Goodbye, Mom. I love you. We all love you."

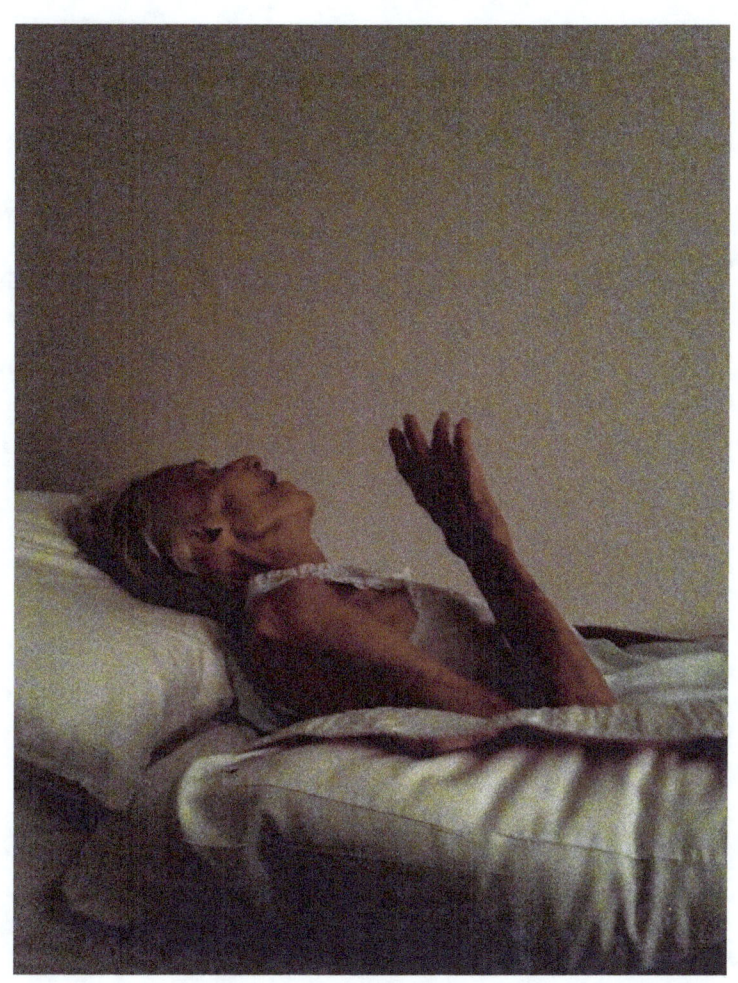

R.I.P. Valentina Natalia Lyczkowski – "Violet Ryder"

Born August 6, 1918 – Died May 26, 2014